THE
PURE
EQUITY
PLUS
PLAN

YOUR PATH TO A
MULTIMILLION-DOLLAR RETIREMENT

PETER J. TANOUS

T0124570

Published by Advantage, Charleston, South Carolina.
Member of Advantage Media Group.

ADVANTAGE is a registered trademark, and the Advantage colophon is a trademark of Advantage Media Group, Inc.

Printed in the United States of America.

10 9 8 7 6 5 4 3 2 1

ISBN: 978-1-64225-288-0
LCCN: 2021915663

Cover design by Carly Blake.
Layout design by Analisa Smith.

This publication is designed to provide accurate and authoritative information in regard to the subject matter covered. It is sold with the understanding that the publisher is not engaged in rendering legal, accounting, or other professional services. If legal advice or other expert assistance is required, the services of a competent professional person should be sought.

Advantage Media Group is proud to be a part of the Tree Neutral® program. Tree Neutral offsets the number of trees consumed in the production and printing of this book by taking proactive steps such as planting trees in direct proportion to the number of trees used to print books. To learn more about Tree Neutral, please visit **www.treeneutral.com**.

Advantage Media Group is a publisher of business, self-improvement, and professional development books and online learning. We help entrepreneurs, business leaders, and professionals share their Stories, Passion, and Knowledge to help others Learn & Grow. Do you have a manuscript or book idea that you would like us to consider for publishing? Please visit **advantagefamily.com**.

For Josephine Tanous and Henry Tanous

CONTENTS

Acknowledgments

The acknowledgments section is a standard part of every published book, and I often wonder who reads them, a question I have asked rhetorically in almost all the books I have written. I suppose, of course, that people who expect to be acknowledged read the pages to see if they were appropriately mentioned, while family members who put up with the author's time away from family activities and his peculiar moods certainly deserve their share of thanks and praise. Yes, I am one of those people who peruse the acknowledgments pages of every book I read, even when I don't know the author personally, fully aware that I will likely not recognize the names of any of the people the author chose to acknowledge. Apparently, you are one of those people too.

So why are we reading these pages? Perhaps we want to be reassured that the author received expert advice on technical matters in subjects where he is not himself an expert, like police procedures, hospital and emergency room protocols, flying airplanes, and the like. I am also curious to see if there are any famous people's names peppered among the acknowledged who might have helped the author along the way. Perhaps the author is recognizing a long-lost love he or she doesn't really want to talk much about. And who are the people the author dedicated the book to, and why?

Now it's my turn: In writing this book, I relied on my fifty-plus years of experience in the stock market and have come to some conclusions that are different from those I held earlier, or even more recently when I wrote books on the subject of investing. "So you changed your mind?" Some might ask this question, and yes, I did. I am reminded of when the famous economist John Maynard Keynes was challenged by a reporter who criticized him for changing his mind about a subject he worked on. Keynes responded: "When the facts change, I change my mind—what do you do, sir?"

The book uses historical data, which was needed to convince readers that the simple investment policy I propose will get them the best possible retirement fortune, with a long history of performance serving as a guide. To gather and analyze this data, I recruited the help of my colleagues at Lynx Investment Advisory here in Washington, DC, and from our colleagues in outposts such as Paris, France, and Casablanca, Morocco. To this end, I am especially grateful to Peter Pavlov, my Paris colleague, whose expertise in financial analysis is at the highest level. Peter's diligence and application to the task were especially helpful to me and gave me the confidence that I was on the right path. Thanks to my colleague Fadoua Arif in Casablanca, who assisted in the research. Fadoua's credentials in finance are augmented by the fact that she is the women's chess champion of North Africa. If you want to play chess with her, I'm taking bets. Thanks to Lynx's CEO, my successor, Vipin Sahijwani, for his expertise.

Are you still reading?

Special thanks to my trophy wife of fifty-eight years, Ann Tanous, who has been through all this before and always offers comfort and wisdom while I have written these books over the years. My children, Chris, Will, and Helene, are always there for me, and I intend to focus on the joys of grandparenthood more and more in future years. Thanks to my son-in-law, Paul Bartilucci, who is the only family member in the financial industry, providing me with an outlet for talking business at family gatherings. And much admiration and appreciation to daughter-in-law Julie Tanous, a celebrated chef, whose cookbook, *Food with Friends*, which she coauthored with actor Jesse Tyler Ferguson, is soaring the charts.

Many thanks and much appreciation to Kate Anslinger, my editor and friend, for her wise and thoughtful edits and comments that gave clarity to sometimes hard-to-read subject matter. Kate is also an accomplished novelist with a devoted following. Check out her latest novel, *Family Photos*. Thanks and kudos to the Advantage publishing team and to Kristin Goodale, Stephen Larkin, and Carly Blake for their excellent work.

A special word of thanks to my dear friend, Jeff Cox, finance editor at CNBC, who wrote the foreword to this book. In addition to being a friend, Jeff and I coauthored two books together, *Debts, Deficits and the Demise of the American*

Economy and *The 30-Minute Millionaire*. Jeff's wisdom is on display both in words and in person on CNBC, where his appearances and his writing on financial matters attract a huge following.

Have I forgotten anyone? Damn. I'm sure I'll think of someone who should have been mentioned when the book goes to press. If you're reading this and I should have mentioned you, I promise I'll make it up to you.

And since you asked (or didn't), the book is dedicated to Josephine Tanous and Henry Tanous, ages seven and four respectively, my most recent grandchildren, who enjoy the good life with their parents, Will and Julie Tanous, in California.

Foreword

Back during the Great Financial Crisis of 2008-09, I was on the lookout for smart people—the type who not only could explain to me what was happening as the global financial system was collapsing, but also what to do next.

Though we had not been acquainted for long, relatively speaking, I knew Peter Tanous to be one of those smart guys.

In the days and weeks and months leading up to the earth-shattering implosion of the investment bank and Wall Street stalwart Lehman Brothers on Sept. 15, 2008, Peter and I had spent hours on the phone discussing the unfolding events.

Peter was always there with a sharp insight, a touch of wit and an unbridled enthusiasm and confidence in the American system that helped me greatly in my reporting for CNBC.com. But he also had a sense of realism about him and knew that what was happening was serious and would change the perspective that many Americans had on investing.

So nine days after Lehman fell, as US authorities launched what would be the most ambitious bailout in the history of the American financial system, I again called on Peter.

Why? Because I knew Peter was smart and he'd have something smart to say that I could share with my readers.

Smart, you say? How smart? Well…this smart.

Here's a quote that appeared Sept. 24, 2008 from Peter under the headline "How to Trade the Bailout: Buy Only the Best in Banks." His quote, though wasn't about just banks but the market in general:

"By many metrics stocks are priced as low as they have been for 25 years. If you still believe in the future of this country, it is very possible that in five years from now you will be able to look back and say, 'Wow, what a buying opportunity.' "

Now look at that quote, made at a time of almost unprecedented peril, and read it again.

Then consider this: Just in those nine days since the Lehman collapse, the S&P 500 had lost more than 5 percent of its value. The index ultimately would plunge another 44 percent from that day when Peter and I spoke, but yet he never lost his confidence that, ultimately and not without some pain, the U.S. market would come back and investors would be made whole again.

Flash forward five years to the day from when that article ran and the S&P 500 was up 43 percent, and that included the massive dive it would take before bottoming in March 2009. Indeed, what a buying opportunity.

The moral of the story: Peter Tanous kept his head during the crisis. He wasn't running around foretelling doom and gloom and telling people to sell everything they owned because catastrophe had hit Wall Street. I knew many, many people who were panicking during the crisis, unable to see any end in sight to the financial contagion. Peter wasn't one of them. Instead, he was doing what any good investor does: Looking through the noise of the present and into the promise of the future, knowing that ultimately America would be back in business.

That's a smart guy.

Of course, we all know now that by Sept. 24, 2013, the market wasn't even halfway through the longest bull market run in history, a time when just being patient and staying the course would have netted even casual investors a tidy sum for their retirement or day-to-day portfolios.

During all that time, Peter and I forged not only a strong professional relationship but also a warm friendship that continues to this day. We've talked investing ideas over Lebanese food in New York's Upper East Side, over steaks near his Washington, DC home, and while enjoying a fine cigar and a glass of scotch on the beaches of the Florida coast.

Oh, and we also wrote a couple of pretty good books together along the way: 2011's *Debt, Deficits and the Demise of the American Economy*, and 2016's *The 30-Minute Millionaire*.

Peter's latest endeavor picks up pretty much where our last book left off.

In "*30-Minute*," we advised investors to stop trying to pick stocks and instead adopt a hybrid passive strategy that included buying funds across a variety of sectors that would provide good equity exposure while not wasting resources on diversification or the low-rent world of bonds.

With the Pure Equity Plus concept, Peter takes that idea and simplifies it even further, offering a reliable, time-tested way for young—and youngish—investors an easy method to achieve their financial goals without even having to put in 30 minutes a week, as our earlier book prescribed.

Despite its criticism from the folks on Wall Street who are getting hit by it, index investing has more than proven itself over the years. As Peter points out in this book, most pros on Wall Street, who've devoted their very lives to the art of stock picking, fail to beat even the most basic benchmarks like the S&P 500, its more concentrated and better-known cousin the Dow Jones Industrial Average, or the various Russell indices.

In a good year, about 40 percent of stock pickers beat the market. Those aren't very good odds, and even worse for you if you're relying on them, and their high fees, to guide you to financial freedom and security.

Peter, though, has a plan. The plan calls for patience, it calls for diligence, but most of all it calls for staying the course even when things don't look so good. That's the kind of approach that has made Peter one of the best at what he does, and it's the kind of approach that will deliver you a prosperous retirement and a road to achieve your other financial goals as well.

It's been my privilege to be associated with Peter, and I strongly believe it will be to your benefit to follow this intelligent, proven way to investment riches.

—*Jeff Cox, CNBC.com*

CHAPTER ONE

Introduction

This short book will tell you how to accumulate a fortune in the stock market for your retirement. We are defining the word *fortune* as a retirement nest egg of at least $1 million and more likely several million dollars. As you have heard countless times, investment professionals are reminded by the US Securities and Exchange Commission (SEC) to advise investors that past performance is no guarantee of future results. This is good advice to heed. But if there are no guarantees, what is the next-best option to assure investment success? For me, a long pattern of success in any given strategy comes as close as possible to ensuring your investments will work for you. The longer the record, the greater our confidence that the investment pattern will continue. Based on that criterion, the investment plan I'm recommending has a track record longer than any other investment plan you will ever encounter. That's a good start.

Before we go on, I'd like to include a word about me, your author and advisor. I have more than fifty years' experience as an investment professional. Over the years, I've made the same mistakes as most investors, and during that time I have gained a lot of knowledge. Much of what I've learned has been regurgitated in the seven investment and economic books that I have authored or coauthored. Twenty years ago, I launched my author career with *Investment Gurus*, which became a best seller, and much of the content is still taught in graduate school courses on investing today. *Investment Gurus* features interviews with top money managers and academics in the investment field, including three Nobel Prize winners in economics. It incorporates a detailed examination of the Efficient Market Theory, which we'll discuss a bit later.

> **The Pure Equity Plus Plan is designed for investors who are fifty years old or younger—the younger the better.**

I must point out early on that the Pure Equity Plus Plan is designed for investors who are fifty years old or younger—the younger the better. The success of this plan relies on time and the value of long-term investing. It offers an easy-to-use, simple, and proven investment plan and comes with the best track record of success.

So why am I writing a book?

You may initially jump to the assumption that I am doing this to make money, and while I hope this book sells millions of copies and consequently helps millions of individuals and families achieve their financial goals, I'm not doing it for the money. In fact, most of the proceeds will go to charity. Thanks to a lifetime spent cracking the code for investment success, I am well off and enjoying a comfortable semiretirement. However, if I had known to follow the recommendations you will find here at a far younger age, I would be much richer than I am today. Fifty years' experience has made me a good deal wiser than I was when I was in my twenties and thirties, and my main goal is to share what I have learned with you.

Before we continue, I want to alert you to what will be the most controversial part of this book, which I will discuss in detail in chapter 4:

the issue of asset allocation. Multiple Nobel Prizes in economics have been awarded for work related to asset allocation and its effect on the risk in investment portfolios. Among the Nobel laureates you will read about is Harry Markowitz, whose Modern Portfolio Theory is widely used by investment professionals in the allocation of investment portfolios. In my book *Investment Gurus,* I interviewed Nobel laureate Bill Sharpe. His Capital Asset Pricing Model (CAPM) addresses stock market risk, and his eponymous Sharpe Ratio is widely used to evaluate risk-adjusted investment performance. I also spoke with Eugene Fama, a more recent Nobel laureate, whose Three Factor Model is an ingenious solution to reducing stock market risk in portfolios through diversification by investment style (growth versus value) and size (large-cap versus small-cap). But here's the problem: What do they mean by *risk*? In this book, I will dissect portfolio risk and prove to you that asset allocation and its effort to reduce risk does more harm than good to long-term investment performance. Backing proof of this with examples I've gathered in my fifty-year career, I will show you that a long-term investor hoping to have a substantial nest egg upon retirement should avoid all asset allocation and diversification advice promulgated by the investment management industry. I will demonstrate that asset allocation is not an investment tool but rather a psychological exercise designed to help you cope emotionally with significant market declines that inevitably occur, although more rarely than most investors think. By reading this book, you will soon understand why asset allocation and diversification will cost you $1 million or more in cash, diminishing your ultimate retirement account. I will then surprise you by sharing that some of the world's greatest investors agree with me, or to put it more modestly and appropriately, I agree with them.

A second controversial aspect of this book will go against another dictum of traditional investment management advice: how often to reexamine your investments. Most advisors want you to keep close track of your investments and follow their progress religiously. I recommend the opposite. Once you have invested in this plan, you need not look at it again ever, or at least not until you are curious to learn how much you have accumulated toward your retirement goal. The exception will be to occasionally rebalance your portfolio holdings, perhaps once a year, but in general, this historically proven plan will need very little supervision or monitoring. Why? Because the stock market will do the work for you.

I call this investment plan the Pure Equity Plus Plan (PEPP). While I could explain in a few pages how to implement PEPP, the purpose of this book is to ignite confidence in you so you have the tools to follow the ideas that I'll be presenting. By offering advice laced with proof, my goal is to help you gain trust that this investment plan will work for you, as you'll soon see that the information provided will go against just about everything you ever knew or were taught about investment management. As I explain the plan in the upcoming pages, we will travel on a journey through the history of investment management, and we will address potential risks that may be encountered along the way. I will acquaint you with some of the investment pioneers, demonstrate how investment risk has changed over the years, and show how these findings have influenced our investing culture, both rightly and wrongly, up until today.

CHAPTER TWO

Let's Talk about Probability and Risk

When you flip a coin, what are the odds it will come up either heads or tails? Everyone knows the answer to that one is 50 percent. So if you flip a coin a hundred times, tails will come up fifty times and heads will come up fifty times, right? Most of us agree that it might work out that way, or it might not. If you try the experiment yourself, you'll end up with a variety of results. Heads may come up sixty times and tails forty times, in one case. In another case, tails might come up fifty-eight times and heads forty-two times. The greater the number of flips, though, the greater the chance that the end result will be close to fifty-fifty.

Now, suppose you enjoy an occasional trip to Las Vegas with the intention of testing your luck at the casino. You pass by a packed roulette wheel that has a light stick showing the number and colors of the last dozen spins. With some excitement, you notice that this particular light stick shows that the color red has come up eight times in a row. You're probably thinking that the next number has to be black, because there is no way those reds will keep coming up. (Let's not even mention the green 0 and 00 numbers.) Of course, you immediately put a stack of chips on black, but what are the chances black will come up on the next spin? The answer, of course, is still fifty-fifty (again, in this example, ignoring those two green numbers). This happens because the roulette wheel in your favorite casino is not blessed with a memory and doesn't really know that it just spun red eight times in a row. With this, we can conclude that the odds on the next spin are no different than on any other spin.

We are referencing coin flipping and roulette numbers to introduce the subject of probability. Because the ancient Greeks didn't have much use for it, probability theory was slow to get off the ground throughout history, yet today every insurance company must deal in probability theory to price a life insurance policy or any other kind of insurance. After all, you need to have some idea of the odds regarding the life expectancy of the insured so that you are prepared to pay the beneficiaries the proper amount while charging a premium that keeps the insurance company in business.

Probability is a function of mathematics, so most of the work done in this field is credited to great mathematicians. For our purposes, we will zero in on those mathematicians who dedicated their time to stock price movements rather than the chances of a monsoon, life expectancy, or games of chance, even though in many cases the theories are related.

As we start the process of building confidence in your new investment strategy, the one that I expect will earn millions for you, we will delve into the history of the various principles we rely on for success.

We start with Carl Friedrich Gauss, who was born in Braunschweig, Germany, in 1777. Gauss was born into a poor working-class family, but his genius became apparent in his very early years. At age three, simply by computing the results in his head, he reportedly corrected a column of numbers his father had been working on. Through a series of fellowships and bolstered by the encouragement of his mother, Gauss landed at the University of Göttingen and soon began to attract attention for his elegant and important mathematical discoveries.

Although Gauss's contributions to the world of mathematics were monumental, his life was a difficult one. In most cases, mathematicians are not gregarious, outgoing people, and Friedrich Gauss was no exception to the rule. After marrying young, his first wife, Johanna, died prematurely in 1809. One of his and Johanna's six children died shortly thereafter, driving Gauss into a deep depression. He subsequently got remarried, to his late wife's best friend, but she died in 1831 after a long illness. After back-to-back tragedies, the broken man was cared for by one of his daughters until his death in 1855.

Friedrich Gauss's difficult personal life did not impede his monumental achievements, and his fame spread all over Europe. In fact, one report stated he was so acclaimed that when troops approached Gauss's town of Göttingen in 1807, they were stopped short under orders from their commander, Napoleon, who spared the city "because the greatest mathematician in history lived there."

Gauss's Latin-written book *Disquisitiones Arithmeticae* made significant contributions to number theory; however, it was his work on statistical distributions that resulted in the Gaussian bell curve that is of most interest to us in the analysis of risk in the stock market. (The original bell curve was developed by French mathematician Abraham de Moivre some eighty years earlier.) Somewhat counterintuitively, the bell curve is used to determine error rather than accuracy and the distance between the two. When we invest in stocks, we might expect to earn a 10 percent return over the years, but since we can't forecast that future return accurately, what we really want to know is how far off our return might be from the 10 percent we expect. This is what is meant by *error*. This leads us into the topic of probability, which takes into consideration the chances of any given circumstance. For example, if you are planning a vacation trip to Hawaii next month, you may want to know what the chances are that it will rain a lot during your trip. If we take a bus trip to Chicago in July, what are the chances the bus might crash? Would we be safer in an airplane? What are the chances of a stock market crash? Gauss used the bell curve to determine these answers.

Even if you've never heard of the term *bell curve*, you may remember talking to your fellow students in high school or college about an exam that was going to be "graded on the curve." Bingo! That was the bell curve, and figure 1 is what it looks like:

FIGURE 1

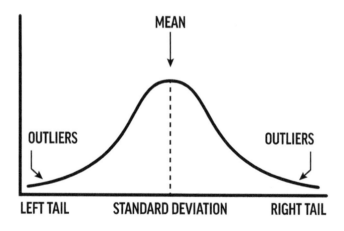

"Grading on the curve" simply meant that the professor was not going to assign a specific grade for each exam based on how many right answers each student got. Instead, since the test was particularly tough, and since most of the students did poorly, he or she might decide to use the curve, which meant distributing the grades around a mean, or an average. So even if all the results were poor, the teacher would give an average grade—a C+, for example—to the ones that were average for the entire group of papers, and then the rest of the grades would be distributed around that average grade or mean. So the ones who were better than the average would get a higher grade, and the ones who were worse would get a lower grade. That meant that even if you didn't do well on the exam but did better than everyone else, you'd get an A.

The bell curve shows the distribution of a number of different phenomena or events. This brings us to stocks. If you consider buying a high-tech-company stock that has a historic range of prices over the last five years of between $4 a share and $125 a share, you would likely agree that this particular stock is volatile given the wide range of its price fluctuations. On the other hand, a different stock, perhaps that of a public utility, only fluctuated between $20 and $30 over the same period. Clearly, the utility stock is much less volatile than the high-tech stock; its price range is much narrower. The changes are measured statistically by something called *standard deviation*. The majority of stocks don't move up or down that much, and those that move around the least represent 68 percent of the total sample of stocks. That 68 percent group is said to be within one standard deviation of the mean. Ninety-five percent of the stocks are within two standard deviations, and 98 percent are within three standard deviations. Using this scale, you can easily see that standard deviations of greater than three are rare events indeed.

Consider another type of distribution: average male heights. Assume the average height of men in the US is five feet eight with a standard deviation of two inches. That means that 68 percent of men are between five feet six and five feet ten inches tall. Ninety-five percent of men are between five feet four and six feet tall; these are the two-standard-deviation measurements. Now we get into rarer territory: three standard deviations. At this level, the men range between short at five feet two and tall at six feet two. The distributions continue on both ends of the bell curve with increasingly rarer results, from those with dwarfism to NBA centers.

Why is this important? There are many reasons. Take the following case, which I used in my book *Investment Gurus*. Suppose you are a rich manufacturer in China and you don't know anything about the US (except that it buys a lot of your little widgets), and you want to take your family on a vacation to America. Since you will be traveling in February, good weather is an important consideration. When you ask your trusty weather app for the average temperature in various US locales, it responds with two places—Minneapolis and Honolulu, each with average temperatures of around seventy-four degrees. "That'll do," you say. And you had better hope you didn't pick lovely Minneapolis for your trip in February.

How come both cities can have the same average year-round temperature? It's all in the distribution. In other words, Honolulu has a very low standard deviation of temperatures, and Minneapolis has a very high standard deviation. Year-round temperatures in Honolulu range from a low of fifty-three degrees to a high of ninety-four degrees. In Minneapolis, the range is much greater, starting at minus thirty-four and ending at 105. Unfortunately, that minus thirty-four degrees is likely to happen during your February vacation.

In later chapters, we'll be discussing the bell curve in greater detail, and you'll learn that the controversy today arises from the use of the bell curve and standard deviation as valid measures of risk in the stock market. Is the distribution of stock movements on the New York Stock Exchange as accurate a sample as the distribution of American male heights or the weather in Hawaii? We'll see. In any event, although we have Gauss to thank for the use of what is now known as the Gaussian bell curve, a statistical process still very much in use today, later analyses will fault the probability statistics thrown off by the bell curve when it comes to extreme stock market events.

When we put money in the bank or buy a US Treasury bill or bond, we get very little return on our money, but we can rest comfortably knowing that we'll get our money back when the bond matures plus the meager interest payments that we were promised. Investors agree that there is no risk of principal loss when we buy a US Treasury security or put money in a bank that is insured by the Federal Deposit Insurance Corporation (FDIC). What if we want to go for a higher return than the bank or the government pays, or maybe we want to invest in the stock market? When we do that, we expect a higher return than what we'll get with those safe bank deposits or government bonds. In exchange for that higher return, we also recognize that we must assume the risk that we might lose money instead. That's the trade-off. If you want absolute investment safety, you'll get a lower return on your money. If you want

We must assume the risk that we might lose money instead. That's the trade-off.

a higher return, you'll have to assume the risk of losing some or even all of it. And thanks to Gauss, we learned how to estimate the amount of risk a particular investment is associated with.

Nobody likes to lose money, and investment advisors hate to tell clients that their portfolios are doing badly, ultimately making these purveyors of investment advice obsessed with risk. In my opinion, over the past decades, the focus on risk has become detrimental to the financial well-being of most American investors. I am going to highlight that detriment as I guide you toward the best path to achieve wealth in the stock market. To get there, it will be useful to gain an understanding of how and why we got to the point of dishing out overly cautious investment advice to clients. The first potential culprit is the Nobel Prize in Economic Sciences.

The History of the Nobel Prize in Economic Sciences

Since economics was not in the original charter for the Nobel Prize, the central bank of Sweden, Sveriges Riksbank, instituted a new award in 1968. "The Sveriges Riksbank Prize in Economic Sciences in Memory of Alfred Nobel" was developed to recognize economic commitment by the bank in perpetuity. The award is given by the Royal Swedish Academy of Sciences and done in accordance with the same principles as the Nobel Prizes that have been awarded since 1901.

More recently, the economics Nobel Prize has gone to finance academics who have devised ways to measure and mitigate risks in investment portfolios. These principles and theories have infused new practices into the investment industry and were designed to reduce stock market risk in managing investments.

Among the most influential of these academics was Harry Markowitz. In the 1940s, when Markowitz was finishing high school in his native Chicago, he earned his undergraduate degree at the University of Chicago and stayed there to pursue his advanced degree in economics. While in Chicago, he had the opportunity to study with Milton Friedman, who became the leader of what would soon be called the Chicago School of Economics. Friedman was perhaps the greatest economist of our times. George Shultz, who was dean of the business school at the time, would subsequently become US secretary of state, and Friedman would become the first of a line of Nobel Prize winners from the University of Chicago. Years later, Harry Markowitz would follow suit, earning the Nobel Prize in economics in 1990.

At a time when most stock market theories concentrated on the expected return on investment, Markowitz decided to focus on the risk investors assumed when they bought stocks. In 1952, the *Journal of Finance* published a short article titled "Portfolio Selection," by Harry Markowitz, then a young graduate student in his midtwenties. This paper contained the principles embodied in what was later to be called Modern Portfolio Theory, which is still very much practiced and revered today. In essence, Markowitz took the position that an investor should consider not just each stock he owned separately but rather the big-picture concept of the portfolio, which should be looked at quite differently than a collection of individual holdings.[1]

In its simplest form, Modern Portfolio Theory is about investment return, investment risk, and investment diversification. Most of us realize intuitively that when we invest in the stock market, we assume some degree of risk, considering stocks can go down and lose money as well as go up and make a profit for the shareholders. If we could get the same return by investing in a safe bank certificate of deposit (CD), why would we bother with the stock market? Unlike the very long odds of gambling on a lottery ticket or a slot machine, the only reason investors are willing to assume the risk of investing in stocks is that they expect a higher return for assuming that risk. Harry Markowitz taught us that by diversifying our various investments across different types of stocks, bonds, and other investments, we can *reduce* our risk and enhance our returns. While this is a great idea, did this elegant new theory really enhance returns?

---

1   Harry M. Markowitz, "Portfolio Selection," *Journal of Finance 7*, no. 1 (March 1952): 77–91.

Think for a moment about the concept of diversification. What's the first expression that comes to mind? My guess is, "Don't put all your eggs in one basket." Now, what exactly is the message conveyed by this common expression? If you are skipping along the path to Grandma's house and you want to bring ten eggs to the family brunch, suppose you happen to slip and fall. All your eggs in that basket would be broken. That's covariance—if the basket falls, all the eggs would wind up broken. Had the load been "diversified" among the other relatives going to brunch, then a single fall would only have destroyed one egg rather than all of them. There is no covariance among baskets being carried along different paths, and their fates are not intertwined.

So, the theory goes, from an investor's point of view, we need to be careful not to put all our eggs in one basket. In the case of a stock portfolio, we must try to own stocks that don't have much covariance (i.e., stocks that don't tend to act in the same manner). If we buy a basket full of tech stocks, for example, they have a lot of covariance, just like the ten eggs in one basket. If tech stocks go down, it is likely that all your stocks will go down, much as all the eggs will get broken if you and your basket suffer a nasty tumble. So you are advised to diversify your portfolio of stocks by buying stocks from different companies in different industries that tend not to behave in lockstep. Likewise, having ten eggs in ten separate baskets is a lot less risky than having ten eggs in one basket. The eggs in the ten baskets have no covariance, and the ten eggs in one basket have a lot of covariance. If a report comes out that retail sales declined, you won't be surprised if most of the retail stocks decline in the aftermath, so you don't want to own a concentration of retail stocks. That's ten eggs in one basket!

Now, this may sound fairly obvious, but the notion of diversification and risk was an earth-shattering discovery in the field of finance. Markowitz went on to write a book, *Portfolio Selection: Efficient Diversification of Investment,* which was essentially his PhD thesis. The book was published in 1959, and the history of investment selection changed forever.[2]

In theory, when an investor buys any stock in the market, he assumes investment risk in the

---

2   Harry M. Markowitz, *Portfolio Selection: Efficient Diversity of Investments* (New York: Wiley, 1959) (Rand Corp., Santa Monica).

form of stock market risk. The stock market moves up and down in an unpredictable fashion, so an investor who wants to make money by buying a stock that he hopes will go up must assume the risk that it might go down. Diversification helps reduce that risk by encouraging the investor to buy many stocks so the risk is spread out over his entire portfolio.

But Markowitz goes on to point out that for diversification to be useful, it has to be the right type of diversification. For example, if you bought not one but ten tech stocks today, you would not have diversified properly, because tech stocks tend to behave similarly as a group, going up and down in sync as the market views the outlook for that sector either positively or negatively. In technical terms, Markowitz suggests that a portfolio should not have stocks with high covariances among themselves. Markowitz referred to the desired collection of assets as an "Efficient Portfolio," which should provide the highest return for the amount of stock market risk an investor is willing to take. But all investors don't have the same investment objective or the same tolerance for risk; therefore, one size won't fit all. When Markowitz realized this, he developed the formulas for calculating the ideal portfolio composition between stocks, bonds, and any other measurable asset class, so that an investor would know the return he or she could expect for any level of risk the investor was prepared to take. He later coined the concept "the Efficient Frontier."

If this sounds familiar, it is likely that you have an investment advisor who prepared a portfolio of assets for you using precisely this concept developed by Markowitz. Indeed, it is more widely used today than ever before, because the calculations required are formidable. In Markowitz's day, computers were primitive and slow, and it took days to perform the thousands of calculations required to produce an efficient frontier for a given portfolio. In many cases, computer time was only available in the middle of the night and, even then, only at a high cost. To get this right, calculating the different possible ranges of each asset's price performance was required. From that point, thousands of different combinations of price performance for each of the stocks or other assets relative to one another were calculated. We know, of course, that now a $500 laptop can perform these calculations in seconds, and that is one reason this type of analysis is so popular in the professional investment community today.

As you read this short history of Markowitz's contribution to investment management, it really is seductive. Thanks to good old Harry and those who followed him, we can have our cake and eat it, too, meaning we can get a positive return from investing in stocks while reducing the risk in investing to a minimum. No wonder the investment industry embraced this concept with sweet kisses and rose-colored glasses.

Now I am about to tell you that the theory doesn't work for most of us. What is missing in this analysis is the answer to this question: If we overemphasize the risk in investing, what are we giving up? By following these principles, we are in fact reducing our future returns substantially to achieve a modest reduction of risk. What's more, we are tailoring our investments to reduce the risk of major stock market declines that happen only a handful of times in a century.

In the coming chapters, I'll show you why this makes no sense if you are an investor with a long time horizon, which is why I stated that this book is intended for investors fifty and younger who have the ability to invest for more than fifteen years. My plan will follow history in getting you to a millionaire's retirement portfolio when you decide to hang up your boots and go out and enjoy yourself.

CHAPTER THREE

To Diversify or Not to Diversify–That Is the Conundrum

In chapter 2, we examined the widely used theory that diversification is an essential component of successful investing, which is what Nobel laureate Harry Markowitz is credited for teaching us. Don't put all your eggs in one basket and all that. The investment advisory crowd has been using this principle for decades; however, the problem lies in the fact that advisors are more concerned with *not losing money* than they are with making money for their clients. I know this because I am one of them. Investment advisors are useful, and they will help you avoid making money-managing mistakes; however, most people don't need a full-time investment advisor until they get rich and have a substantial portfolio on which to retire. By the time you need an advisor, you will likely be nearing retirement age, and the role of your advisor will be to help ensure that your fortune stays intact.

If you are just starting out, you may be able to forgo the advisor and simply follow the proven tips in this book. But first, ask yourself if the Pure Equity Plus Plan is the right approach for you. Follow that up with these questions: "Should I diversify my investments as I build a long-term nest egg? Is diversification and Modern Portfolio Theory the right way to get rich?"

You already know what I think, so let's listen to somebody more qualified than me on this subject. Warren Buffett has been quoted saying the following:

> *We think diversification, as practiced generally, makes very little sense for anyone who knows what they're doing.*

Diversification is a protection against ignorance.

Warren Buffett said the above at the 1996 Berkshire Hathaway annual meeting of shareholders. He was responding to a question from one of the audience members.

To be clear, the above quotes were in response to a question about why Berkshire Hathaway had such a concentrated portfolio of stocks rather than owning many more. But the general point Buffett makes about diversification applies to the Pure Equity Plus Plan as well.

Then there is this quote, with which I not only agree but also find the humor Buffett injects an added bonus:

> *Modern Portfolio Theory has no utility. It will tell you how to do average. You can do average in fifth grade. [Modern Portfolio Theory] is elaborate. There's lots of little Greek letters and all kinds of things to make you think you're in the big leagues. But there is no value added.*

Maybe the wrong guy won the Nobel Prize.

There are many more quotes like this from Buffett and his partner Charlie Munger, but no need to pile on. Buffett and Munger are talking about their approach to investing from the viewpoint of Berkshire Hathaway, and the principles they espouse can serve us all well. As Charlie Munger once put it, "Diversification is for the know-nothing investor."

Let's go over the message here. I maintain that asset allocation, diversification, and Modern Portfolio Theory are investment philosophies that are designed to protect the portfolio manager and the investment advisor more so than the client, who is investing his or her savings. As you just read, I'm in good company in thinking that way. So why do so many investment professionals live by these questionable theories? Are they smarter than Warren Buffett? Certainly not. The reason they latch on to these principles is that your investment advisor doesn't want to relive the stock market experiences of 2000–2001 (the dot-com bubble) or

> **Asset allocation, diversification, and Modern Portfolio Theory are investment philosophies that are designed to protect the portfolio manager and the investment advisor more so than the client.**

2008–2009 (the financial near collapse). These were times when advisors were forced to tell their clients that their portfolio had declined 40 percent simply because they were invested in stocks. Many clients fired their advisors when those calamities occurred, accusing them of not using their expertise to forecast the significant collapses: "You're the professional. You should have known this was going to happen. I've got a friend whose broker told him to sell everything just before the market crashed." Along with every other investment professional, I heard those exact words repeatedly.

From that moment on, the solution for our industry was simply to diversify, making sure all clients had portfolios that reduced volatility by having a mix of noncorrelating asset classes. To simplify, this means that your assets are designated in such a way that they don't correlate, and in turn, they do not go up and down at the same time. You accomplish this by buying bonds, some commodities, and other types of investments. While bonds offer little in the way of return on your investments, they are safe and won't lose much of their value when the market tanks, providing you with a sense of security and less alarm if your stock investments fall. That's a good thing, right?

The premise of this book is that it isn't. There is a better way.

Based on the Pure Equity Plus Plan, I want you to be fully invested in the stock market from the moment you start investing and for the next fifteen to twenty years or longer. While there will be some variations in the recommended portfolio, it's important to remember that it will have zero bonds and will be exposed to serious market declines. My job is to convince you that the heavy exposure is not only justified but also the only way for you to accumulate a fortune before you retire—and I, as a professional with fifty years' experience, am obligated to prove that to you. Given the long history of stock market behavior, which works in our favor, I hope and expect to instill in you the confidence you will need to invest this way.

When you start a relationship with a broker or investment advisor, you will be quizzed on your goals, which is done to assess your risk tolerance. Known as one of the most widely used terms in the industry, *risk tolerance* is measured by your responses to these quiz questions. Your advisor will ask you something like "How would you feel if your portfolio declined by 20 percent in any given year?" This will likely be in the form of a multiple-choice question with answers ranging from "I wouldn't mind at all" to "I'd go out and shoot myself." (Maybe not in those exact words.) The advisor will use this information to tailor the asset allocation of your holdings. If you said something like "A 20 percent loss is acceptable but will cause me some sleepless nights," she is going to tailor your portfolio conservatively, because she doesn't really want you to have any sleepless nights. Therefore, your proposed portfolio will be heavily oriented toward "safe" assets like high-grade bonds, preferred stocks, and investments that are less volatile than most common stocks. That way, when you meet for your quarterly review, she'll tell you that despite some market fluctuations, you haven't lost any money this year. The problem is that you haven't made much money either. For example, in a year when the stock market has risen, say, 25 percent, your portfolio may only have increased by 8 percent, because your exposure to the stock market was limited. On the other hand, if at the quarterly meeting you learn that the stock market has *declined* by 22 percent, she will proudly tell you that as a result of her prudent investment management, your portfolio has only declined by 11 percent. Her goal is to make you feel better. So, don't you feel better?

This is the way the business works, and if you've had a relationship with an investment advisor, I'm confident you won't disagree with what I've just said. Here's where it gets tricky. Investment advisors have the dual responsibility of tailoring a portfolio for you that will grow in value over the years while at the same time protecting you against major losses and sleepless nights. How do you measure whether she has done a good job completing these tasks for you?

Portfolios need to be measured against benchmarks. If your portfolio was invested 100 percent in the US stock market, you might want to use the S&P 500 Index, one of the most commonly followed equity indexes, which measures the stock performance of the five hundred largest companies listed on stock exchanges in the United States. Professional investors consider this a more representative index of the overall market, since the older Dow Jones Industrial Average measures only thirty stocks.

Did you do better than the index, about the same, or worse? Now, if your portfolio is only 60 percent invested in stocks and 40 percent in an array of bonds, you will need to create a custom benchmark that looks similar to your portfolio. In this case, your benchmark might be a combination of two indexes where 60 percent of the benchmark will be measured against the S&P 500 (to measure your stock performance) and the remaining 40 percent in a bond index (to measure your bond performance).

By checking your results, you'll be able to evaluate the level of advice you're getting. Your advisor may have relied on her research department to determine which stocks and bonds she decided to put in your portfolio. You need to resolve whether her selections beat the S&P 500, because she is likely charging you a fee of up to 1 percent for managing your money. If the stock portion of your portfolio isn't beating the stock index, you have a problem, because you can buy that stock index instead of having her pick stocks for you. And the cost of an index will be about ten basis points, or one-tenth of the fee she is charging. You'll need to ask yourself the same question for the bond performance. Did your bonds equal or beat the bond index?

The investment industry wants you to believe that asset allocation is an important investment decision. It isn't. We'll explain why in the next chapter.

CHAPTER FOUR

The Myth of Asset Allocation

A sset allocation is a more sophisticated version of diversification. In the previous chapter, Warren Buffett helped us understand that diversification can hurt rather than help your investment returns.

In the investment business, asset allocation is considered an investment decision; however, it should be viewed as a *psychological* decision. When asked if asset allocation will improve your investment performance, your advisor will likely respond with a tepid answer. "Well, not exactly, but it will help the stability of your portfolio and reduce its volatility" is a common one.

"Okay," you say. "But if it isn't going to make me richer, what's the point?"

"Oh, the reason it's important for you is that it will mitigate declines in the stock market. What if the stock market crashes and goes down 40 percent? That has happened, you know. And what if you need the money right after the market crash? It won't be there, because the value has gone down."

"I guess that's true," you'll say. "But I told you this money is for retirement. I won't need it for another twenty years or so, so I can wait for the recovery."

"That's good to hear," she says. "But we must be careful. If you lost 40 percent as a result of a market calamity, then we didn't do a very good job protecting your assets."

"Hmm ... so the asset allocation process is about you not looking bad? I get it. But it doesn't help my money grow, so forgive me if I'm a bit confused."

While you'll see truth in her statement, the fact that you won't need the money for another twenty years or so is not lost on you, and you're well aware that you'll have plenty of time to await the recovery. Again, she cautions you to be careful, reciting the chance of a 40 percent drop due to a market calamity and the importance of *protecting* your assets.

As you can see here, the asset allocation process is more about the advisor not looking bad and less about your money growing into a notable nest egg.

Before you fly off the handle in frustration, try to refrain. Your advisor is doing everything right, and having taken the investment oath like all her colleagues, she is doing her job to prevent your assets from being harmed, and a 40 percent drop would be considered *a lot of harm*. By being conservative, she will help you avoid market disasters, but the backlash is that you will not maximize your potential gains. As you can see, this is all psychological. What if, after a major decline in your assets, you give up and panic out of the market? While this is the worst-case scenario, this is exactly what your advisor is trying to prevent.

By the end of this book, I hope that you will be an informed investor armed with a solid under-standing of the stock market, holding tightly to the fact that stocks are the only path to financial growth over a long period of time. You'll also know that the market can be choppy and that stocks go down as well as up, but the long-term stock market trend is always up. In fact, stocks rise two-thirds of the time.

I understand that those huge declines of 40 percent or more can be scary, and what your advisor is really worried about is her reputation and whether your portfolio looks good or bad. What she didn't tell you is that she's afraid you will fire her if there is a huge decline in your assets. To make matters worse, she fears you will follow that up by lamenting her poor work to anyone who will listen, ultimately diminishing her credibility. To be fair, that's what many investors do when the going gets rough. So, to prevent client disdain, advisors make it their top priority to make sure your portfolio doesn't get annihilated. In a 40 percent or greater market decline, your nicely diversified portfolio is going to lose money too; there's no avoiding that outcome. But if the decline is much less severe as a result of your broker's cautious approach, you will feel

> **The market can be choppy and stocks go down as well as up, but the long-term stock market trend is always up.**

somewhat protected. And the market will come back, because it always does.

By this point, you may be curious about where the obsession with asset allocation derived from. As you read earlier, Harry Markowitz's Modern Portfolio Theory was a big influence. Then in 1986 came the now-famous Brinson, Hood, and Beebower report, more frequently referred to as BHB.

These three gentlemen dissected the many roles involved in asset allocation that contribute to investment performance. One of those factors is timing and the relationship between advisor and market predictions. Having an advisor who happens to be privy to the rise and fall of the market would be ideal for most investors, which is why BHB wanted to discover how much market timing impacted investment performance.

What about selection talent? Some fund managers seem to have a magical knack for picking stocks that consistently rise. The question then becomes, How much does stock selection affect your returns?

Based on the determined roles of investment performance, the BHB gentlemen launched a study designed to answer just how much weight the asset allocation decision has on determining investment performance.

To get the answers, BHB examined the performance of ninety-one pension funds from 1974 to 1983. They looked at the differences in asset allocation among the various funds and how performance varied from one fund to another. After analyzing the different factors, they found surprising results. Brilliant market timing only accounted for about 7 percent of performance. The study found that 91.5 percent of a portfolio's return was attributable to its mix of assets—that is, diversification or asset allocation. Moreover, the study was done again in 1991, and the results were similar, thereby confirming the validity of the earlier findings.[3]

The investment industry jumped on these findings and in many cases misinterpreted them in chasing after new clients, leading asset allocation to become the bible of investment management. Like the study said, get the asset allocation right, and your risk-adjusted return will be just fine.

---

3   Gary P. Brinson, L. Randolph Hood, and Gilbert L. Beebower, "Determinants of Portfolio Performance," *Financial Analysts Journal* 42, no. 4 (July–August 1986): 39–44. Published by: Taylor & Francis, Ltd.

With that said, let's focus on the term *risk adjusted*.

This term takes us back to your advisor's obsession with asset allocation and her knowing that it doesn't result in earning the most money. What it does is smooth out the returns by chopping off the highs and lows of your investment performance. So *risk adjusted* is a way to balance the risk, by reducing the extremes of your portfolio's performance. It also means that your returns will be considerably lower than they would be if you just stayed in the stock market through the ups and downs. History backs this up and has proven that when the stock market hits all-time highs, which is pretty often, your investment in stocks goes up to new heights.

What if an investor, upon witnessing a decline of 40 percent or more, panicked and sold everything that was left in his portfolio? He would miss the expected recovery, which history tells us invariably comes. And that is the real conundrum, which is precisely what your advisor is trying to keep you from doing by allocating your investments more conservatively. So let's recognize that this is more of a psychological dilemma rather than an investment issue. This may be why Nobel

Prizes in economics have been given recently to economists whose work is in behavioral sciences, not pure economics. These include Richard H. Thaler at the University of Chicago and Robert J. Shiller at Yale, who showed that mass psychology, herd behavior, and the like can have an enormous effect on stock prices. So perhaps the market isn't quite so efficient after all.

Let's face it: if you are like most investors, a major decline in the value of your portfolio is going to have some serious emotional effects on your well-being. Imagine saving up for a number of years and in one fell swoop you see a huge chunk of your hard-earned money go up in smoke. That would be devastating to anyone. However, I am strongly advocating that you assume that risk if your time horizon is a long one, which is why this book is geared toward investors under fifty. History tells us that the stock market always recovers, and patience over time will lead you to that thriving nest egg. We are talking about a very long history, one that dates back to the Great Depression in the 1930s. You simply need to be convinced that after a major decline you will recover, and once you accept that notion, you can tailor your portfolio for maximum gain, which is precisely what we are going to do with the Pure Equity Plus Plan.

CHAPTER FIVE

Analyzing the Major Stock Market Declines

Experts generally believe that a 40 percent stock market decline is the turning point at which panic sets in for most investors. This is the level where a bear market roars and sends a horde of investors to the door. A few brave ones stick around and hunt for bargains, but for most of us, a decline of that magnitude produces a sickening emotional reaction.

So let me ask you this: How often do you think a decline of that magnitude occurs? Every three years? Every five years? Ten years? The truth is, it's not any of those, and likely less often than you think. In fact, since the Great Depression, there have been only three occasions when the stock market declined, peak to trough, by 40 percent or more. Surprised? Most people think there have been many more occasions than that. But there are just three.

Here they are.

1973–1974

To fully understand the crash of 1973–1974, let's take a glimpse at the summer of 1944. The war was still raging in Europe and Japan when finance ministers and delegates from forty-four Allied nations gathered at a bucolic resort in Bretton Woods, New Hampshire, to create a system of monetary policies that would govern the financial relations among free states after the war had ended. The conference created the International Monetary Fund (IMF) and the International Bank for Reconstruction and Development (IBRD, now part of the World Bank). Each nation was to adopt a monetary policy that set exchange rates among countries within 1 percent by tying its currency to gold while giving the IMF the ability to make loans when needed, bridging the temporary balance of payment gaps. The United States, which held two-thirds of the world's gold, insisted that the system be based on both gold and the US dollar. This discipline would prevent member nations from yielding to the temptation to run the printing press any time their balance of payments or deficits got out of whack. The United States would guarantee to redeem dollars from any member nation at thirty-five dollars an ounce. Thus was born the Bretton Woods Agreement based on the gold standard.

By 1971, the United States was fighting inflation. In reaction, many European countries exercised their right to convert their dollars into gold, as allowed by the Bretton Woods Agreement. Because a run on the dollar might have depleted US gold reserves, President Richard Nixon unilaterally canceled the dollar's convertibility into gold in August 1971, a move the Japanese dubbed the "Nixon Shock." The US then instituted wage and price controls to tamp down inflation. The result of the move was to end the era of fixed exchange rates and inaugurate the onset of floating exchange rates. It would soon send the Bretton Woods Agreement up in smoke.

While the move was quite popular at the time, business leaders worried. I recall vividly a conversation at the time with the CEO of a large manufacturing company, who said, "How can I build a new plant in Europe with floating exchange rates, since I won't know what my final cost is going to be?"

The next crisis to hit was the oil embargo. In 1973, members of the Organization of Arab Petroleum Exporting Countries declared an oil embargo as retaliation for the US and European support for Israel during the Yom Kippur War. Since most of the world's oil came from the Middle East, the price of oil skyrocketed from three dollars a barrel to twelve dollars a barrel, adding to the inflationary pressures in the US. Those of you who, like me, are "of a certain age" will remember the very long lines at gas stations during that period. In the two years from 1972 to 1974, the American economy slowed from 7.2 percent real GDP growth to a –2.1 percent contraction, while inflation jumped from 3.4 percent in 1972 to 12.3 percent in 1974.

The stock market took notice. From January 1973 to December 1974, the Dow Jones Industrial Average lost 45 percent of its value, giving us the first 40 percent stock market decline since the end of the Great Depression. The Dow was around 900 before the crash, dropped to around 600, and was back up at the 900 level in 1976.

2000–2001

Arthur Rock is one of the legends in venture capital. I interviewed him for my book *Investment Visionaries* in 2002. Some venture capitalists luck out with a single major investment that turns a few thousand dollars into millions. But in Rock's case, he was an original financier of both Apple and Intel. That takes more than luck. He told me about the first time he met Steve Jobs: "Here's a seventeen- or eighteen-year-old kid; he comes in with a goatee and mustache and had hair down to his shoulders, you know. His clothes probably hadn't been cleaned in two or three weeks." I guess you could say that meeting the teenage Steve Jobs was quite an experience.

I mention Arthur Rock for something else he said during our interview. He made the point that there is a major, life-changing technological development every fifty years. From 1850 to 1900, it was the engine that fostered the Industrial Revolution, automobiles, powered boats, and so on. Then, from 1900 to 1950, it was electricity and all the things that derived from it. From 1950 to 2000, the transistor. Later on, he wondered what the major development in the period beginning in 2000 would be, until it dawned on him: the internet.

At the dawn of the Information Age and what became known as information technology, it quickly became apparent that the internet was going to revolutionize the world we know, so any company that was going to adopt it was going to be a sure-fire investment. Welcome to the dot-com age, and to the dot-com bubble.

In the environment of the late 1990s, anything with a dot-com suffix attracted masses of investors. Dot-com companies went public with scarcely any revenue, much less a profit, while greedy investors piled in. Profits were referred to as a "quaint idea."

Between 1995 and 2000, the Nasdaq Composite Index rose 400 percent. For the January 1999 Super Bowl XXXIII telecast (I'll save you some time—that's thirty-three), two dot-com companies purchased ads. The following year, sixty ads for dot-coms (depending on how you count) were bought for Super Bowl XXXIV (yes, thirty-four) for about $2 million a pop for thirty seconds. Most of the companies that sprang for these expensive ads had no earnings at all.

In time, it became fairly obvious that these heralded companies were burning through cash at an alarming rate with no profits in sight to offset the losses. That led to wake-up time. On March 24, 2000, the S&P 500 Index reached its all-time high of 1,552. Seven months later, most internet stocks had declined 75 percent from their highs, wiping out nearly $1.8 trillion in value. In November, Pets.com, a highflier backed by Amazon, went bust just nine months after its initial public offering. In January 2001, there were just three dot-com advertisers for Super Bowl XXXV (never mind).

Party over.

It took until November 2007 for the S&P 500 to regain its old high of 1,552. But, as always, the market recovered.

2007–2009

In the summer of 2011, I attended a corporate board meeting in Paris accompanied by my wife and our granddaughter, Olivia, who was then ten years old. One beautiful evening, we went to the

Tuileries Garden, where a summer carnival was in full swing. We decided to take Olivia on an amusement park ride. While we queued up to buy the tickets for the ride, I noticed a familiar face ahead of me with his family, negotiating with the booth attendant who spoke no English. Given that I am fluent in French, I stepped up to offer assistance and noticed that the man trying to buy tickets was indeed American, and it was Senator Chris Dodd. When he thanked me for helping out, I mentioned that I lived in Washington and recognized him, and I referred to an occasion when we had met previously. Senator Dodd was extremely pleasant, and we had a brief conversation. Dodd said he thought the attendant sounded irritated and wondered if it was because he was unable to converse in French. I thought for a minute, and unable to resist, I said, "No, Senator—he was just trying to tell you that the Dodd-Frank Bill almost ruined his business." We both had a good laugh, and a few years later, when seated together at a dinner, I reminded him of the story, and we laughed about it again.

In fact, after the financial crisis of 2007–2008, the *Dodd-Frank Wall Street Reform and Consumer Protection Act* (usually referred to as the Dodd-

Frank Act) helped bring an end to the great crisis and instituted reforms on the banking system. It also created a wave of rules and regulations to protect consumers. Many of these reforms were rolled back under the Trump administration.

Not all economists and bankers agree on the cause of the financial crisis of 2007–2009, but they all agree on one word to describe a big part of the crisis: *housing*. It all started in 2000 when the Federal Reserve began lowering interest rates to help avoid a recession caused by the dot-com crash that we described earlier. In fact, interest rates declined dramatically from mid-2000 to December 2001, from 6.5 percent to 1.75 percent. You don't need an advanced degree in economics to figure out what happened next. Just as the Fed wanted, consumer borrowing increased, thanks to the low rates, and the economy recovered. The biggest beneficiary of the lower interest rates was the housing industry. To make housing even more affordable, bankers and mortgage brokers sold loans with balloon payments and very low initial monthly payments. These so-called *adjustable-rate mortgages* (ARMs) offered the borrower a low interest rate pegged to the very low Fed Funds rate, after which the entire principal amount of the loan was due. The marginal borrowers could afford the initial monthly payments so long as the Fed kept interest rates at rock-bottom levels. But if interest rates rose, so would the monthly payments.

In a feat of financial engineering, investment banks "securitized" packaged mortgages, creating mortgage-backed securities (MBSs) and selling chunks of them to institutional investors and hedge funds, who were eager to get the income and principal from these packaged mortgages.

As demand mounted, mortgages were granted to less-qualified borrowers, people with little or no credit. This new class of securities earned the moniker *subprime mortgages* and were the first to default when the crisis began to unravel. Imagine—a family buys a house, takes out a 90 to 95 percent mortgage, but the house price doesn't keep rising; it starts to decline. To the distress of many mortgage holders, starting in 2004 the Fed reversed course and over a two-year period raised rates from 1.25 percent back up to 5.25 percent, marking the start of a major crisis to come. Since most of the mortgage loans were at variable rates, most of the subprime borrowers and many of the homeowners who bought with very little down experienced a surge in their monthly mortgage payments. That provided the perfect storm for a financial disaster. Simply put, many homeowners could no longer afford the monthly payments.

To compound the impending disaster, the housing market had reached a saturation point. Starting in 2006, the housing market peaked, and home sales and prices began to decline. Many subprime mortgage holders were unable to get out from under by borrowing, refinancing, or selling their homes because many mortgage holders now owed more on their loans than their homes were worth.

Now many of the homeowners were *underwater*, as the term went. Having no other way out, homeowners woke up en masse, packed their belongings, and took off, leaving the house keys in the mailbox for the bankers to collect.

As more and more subprime borrowers defaulted, those mortgage-backed securities so eagerly bought by the hedge funds started to go up in smoke. The effect was dramatic on the financial stability of many banks and investment firms, not only in the US but around the world and especially in Europe, spreading the financial crisis around the globe.

In 2007, the financial bubble began to burst with a cascade of bankruptcies and defaults. New Century Financial Corp., one of the largest subprime lenders, filed for bankruptcy, and others soon followed. In August 2007, another large American firm, American Home Mortgage Investment Corporation, declared bankruptcy.

By the summer of 2008, Fannie Mae (the Federal National Mortgage Association) and Freddie Mac (the Federal Home Loan Mortgage Corporation), the huge federally chartered corporations that controlled the secondary mortgage market, incurred enormous losses and faced bankruptcy. The US Treasury Department decided it had no choice but to rescue them. They nationalized both corporations and fired their boards of directors. This operation alone cost the Treasury some $1.5 trillion. Then, in an event that brought even greater shock to the system, the venerable investment bank Lehman Brothers, with over $600 billion in assets, filed the largest bankruptcy in US history.

A series of hastily enacted rescue packages passed Congress and were immediately signed into law by President George W. Bush. By the time the financial crisis had ended, the Treasury had pumped over $4 trillion into the US economy to save it.

In my more than fifty years' experience in observing the stock market, 2007–2009 was by far the scariest, most dramatic episode of financial catastrophe since the Great Depression. I believe I can safely predict that it is highly unlikely we will experience as severe a financial crisis again. We know better, or I think we do. With that said, it should come as no surprise that during this frightful period, we also experienced the worst stock market performance since the Great Depression in the 1930s. In case you forgot, here are the statistics. On October 9, 2007, the S&P 500 Index stood at 1,565. On March 9, 2009, the decline ended and the S&P 500 Index closed at 677 points, a decline of 888 points, or 57 percent. Roughly four years later, the market was back at a new high.

Many of our senior readers will wonder why I didn't discuss the famous stock market crash of 1987. On October 19, 1987, which became known as Black Monday, the Dow Jones Industrial Average fell by 508 points, or 22.6 percent. To this day, that was the largest percentage drop in a single day in history. The reason I didn't mention it is that the recovery from the crash was rapid, and as most people tend to forget, the stock market actually finished positive in 1987, with the Dow Jones Industrial Average gaining 0.6 percent for the year.

Another question: While major stock market declines are unpredictable and rarer than most people think, what if they occur just a few years apart? Now, that's a good question, and as it turns out, that's precisely what happened with the last two meltdowns. The 2000-2001 crash was followed only seven years later by the 2008–2009 crash. So what if an investor started investing just before the 2000–2001 decline? Where would he be after enduring that meltdown and the one that followed just a few years later?

We decided to test the hypothesis of staying invested through thick and thin. As we've just seen, the worst possible time to start investing in the US stock market in recent times would have been just before the two major crashes in 2000–2001 and 2008–2009, staying invested through both crashes. How much would you have lost if you'd stayed invested until now?

For our purposes, we use the S&P 500 as a proxy for the stock market.

So, on December 31, 1998, our hapless investor decided to plunk his life savings, and his future, into the stock market with a solemn promise to stay invested until his retirement some twenty-five years later. We observed the value of the index on January 1, 1999, and assumed our investor kept his promise and stayed invested through two of the most horrible stock market periods in history.

We checked his results on December 31, 2020. On the day he invested at the end of 1998, the S&P 500 Index stood at 1,229. On December 31, 2020, the index was 3,756.

Our investor's portfolio, far from losing money, had increased 365 percent (dividends reinvested). But at what psychological cost? During this period, our investor would have had to endure a peak-to-trough market decline of 50 percent in 2000–2001 and a peak-to-trough decline of 53 percent in 2008–2009 (dividends reinvested, this becomes –45.5 percent and –50.7 percent, respectively).

Few investors can endure that level of pain.

So history suggests that the single best way to make a great deal of money is to invest in the stock market for the long term. We've all heard that said for decades, but even if I can demonstrate convincingly that for an investor under fifty years old, a portfolio invested 100 percent in the S&P 500 Index will serve very well, no one believes it and no one follows that advice. That is precisely the problem we need to correct.

There have been decades when the market returned little or nothing and decades when the annual returns were in the teens. To cite a few examples, if you invested in the index between 2010 and 2019, your total return would be a gain of 256 percent, or 13.5 percent annualized. This is the kind of return most investors would dream of.

The purpose of this book is to convince you that you must stay invested during your entire working life. Look at your retirement portfolio at most once a year, and rebalance your holdings. Do not be afraid of market declines, large or small. They come with the territory. One hundred years of market history have proven that you will retire with a small or large fortune no matter when you start to invest if you just follow the simple plan I outline for you in this book.

Do not be afraid of market declines, large or small. They come with the territory.

Rather than end this chapter on a depressing note, it's fun to recall that in 2010 the very talented writer Michael Lewis wrote a best-selling book about the financial crisis titled *The Big Short: Inside the Doomsday Machine.* The book explained the financial crisis of 2007–2009 and included some colorful characters who actually figured it out and made a ton of money betting against the housing market. Later on, in 2015, director Adam McKay gave the world the film *The Big Short,* starring Christian Bale, Steve Carell, Ryan Gosling, and Brad Pitt. The film attempted the herculean task of explaining the crisis in terms of mortgage-backed securities, collateralized debt obligations, credit default swaps, and other weird and arcane terms that were part of the sausage-making machinery that helped fuel the crisis. Amazingly, and with a good deal of ingenuity, the film succeeded. A technique McKay used was to have unique and well-known personalities explain some of these odd features of finance directly to the film's audience. In one scene, the beautiful actress Margot Robbie explains subprime loans while luxuriating in a bubble bath, drinking champagne. Yes, she got most viewers' attention.

CHAPTER SIX

Fractal Geometry, Black Swans, and Fat Tails

I n this chapter, I want to explain why fear of market crashes has grown disproportionately in recent years, thanks to new theories about risk, standard deviation, and the accuracy of the Gaussian bell curve. These new theories explain why investors and investment advisors are so concerned about catastrophic stock market declines and why you, as a long-term investor saving for your multimillion-dollar retirement, shouldn't be. Some of the information I will share with you might come under the more-than-you-need-to-know category, but my theory is that the more time and energy you spend learning about market risk, the more confidence you'll have in a successful retirement plan.

Benoit Mandelbrot was a French mathematician. He was born in Warsaw, and his family moved to France from Poland when they accurately predicted the coming threat to Jewish families posed by the rising Nazi Party in Germany in the 1930s. Mandelbrot studied in France and was admitted to the prestigious École Polytechnique in the late 1940s. He subsequently studied at the California Institute of Technology, then went back to France and earned a PhD in mathematics at the University of Paris. In 1958, he and his wife moved to the United States, and Mandelbrot joined the research staff at IBM, where he remained for thirty years. He subsequently joined the faculty at Yale as a professor in mathematics.

Mandelbrot was a superb mathematician, and his theories are of special interest to many members of the financial community. Indeed, Mandelbrot is fundamentally changing how we look at risk in the stock market. He is the father of what is known as *fractal geometry*. This is admittedly a complicated form of math in both practice and theory, so we'll try to boil it down to the fundamentals of what this branch of math does. Then we'll explain why it has become so important to the analysis of risk in the stock market.

When we study shapes, forms, and patterns, we look for symmetry. Geometry is a good example with its squares, rectangles, triangles, and other forms that no matter their size follow uniform patterns of construction. The fractal view of the world assumes that patterns of phenomena or even objects in the world are not "stable" and do not follow a neatly ordered structure or pattern. Now, what is interesting about all this to us investors is that when we look at risk using the Gaussian bell curve we discussed earlier, we are, in fact, showing probability along a neat distribution where the most frequent occurrences are found at the center of the bell curve and the rarer events, the "outliers," fall neatly at the extremes to the right and left.

But Mandelbrot looked at the world differently. If you look at the coast of England from a satellite, it looks orderly and linear. But as you get closer, you notice the cliffs and rocks, the shifting coastlines and beaches, and all kinds of craggy land following no pattern at all. Another example: When you see a tree, you instantly know it's a tree even though you have never seen this particular tree before. In fact, this tree looks like most other trees of the same variety. Yet its leaves and branches have a particular pattern that forms a little tree with branches off its main stem, and of course the tree itself has a trunk with branches that shoot off its base form. It doesn't take long to conclude that all trees are different.

You may well conclude that these observations are hardly mind bending, and the fact that trees and coastlines follow irregular shapes is not a difficult concept to grasp. Our own observations readily confirm these facts. What you need to keep in mind is that this irregular and unpredictable pattern of phenomena is important to understand in the context of our estimates of future events and, in our case, what might happen to the stock market. Have another look at the bell curve in figure 2:

FIGURE 2

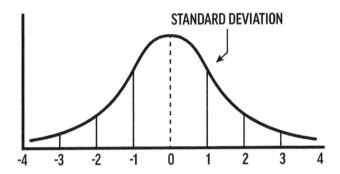

Source: Lynx Investment Advisory.

This time we have added the standard deviation lines on this neatly shaped bell curve. You can see that the curve doesn't accommodate much more than three standard deviations. A three-standard-deviation event is rare indeed— one in one hundred.

The main debate that Mandelbrot has sparked is that market crashes and other investment phenomena that may cost us our life savings are far more likely occurrences than existing investment theories have suggested. This is indeed earth shaking. Nassim Nicholas Taleb, a brilliant mathematical investor/philosopher, wrote a hugely popular best-selling book titled *The Black Swan*, based partially on the work of Benoit Mandelbrot, to whom his book is dedicated. In his provocative and lively book, Taleb points out that it is what we don't know that is far more relevant to our lives and fortunes than what we do know or think we know. It is about the unexpected nature of randomness. (In fact, his earlier book, titled *Fooled by Randomness*, was also a best seller, as were his subsequent books *AntiFragile* and *Skin in the Game*, which I highly recommend.) If you haven't read Nassim Taleb, do yourself a favor and indulge in a fresh take on a number of philosophical and practical issues by one of the sharpest minds in the world today.

The title *The Black Swan* refers to the fact that for centuries we assumed that all swans were white. Indeed, no one had ever seen a black swan, so it was a pretty safe bet. And that was true until Australia was discovered and, with it, its population of black swans. Now, this is hardly a major history-shaking discovery, but it illustrates the importance of being open minded with respect to our judgments and conclusions based simply on our own observations. Mandelbrot's fractal geometry is not about similarity but about "roughness." And the bell curve that is widely used in financial analysis today is neat, symmetrical, and anything but rough.

By contrast, Harry Markowitz's theory appears simpler and easier to grasp. With it, the investment return outlook for your entire portfolio depends on two numbers based on reward and risk or, in statistical terms, mean and variance along with the covariance (the tendency to perform similarly) of the different asset classes your portfolio may hold. With this construct, you can estimate the return you might get over time from your portfolio along with the statistical odds of actually getting your expected return. Pretty neat. How do you do this? You estimate the growth of your stock portfolio using, perhaps, the long-term return on stocks over many decades. Then you analyze the volatility of your portfolio by looking at how much each of the groups of holdings fluctuated over the past years. For example, if you own small-cap stocks and this asset class moved up or down by an average of 15 percent a year over the past ten years, you will assume that the trend in volatility is likely to continue. So we calculate the range of returns of all the asset classes in your portfolio over the next five years on the bell curve (figure 3). The calculations incorporate thousands of different combinations of possibilities, worst case to best case, over a five-year period, aided by the power of today's modern computers. When the probabilities are all calculated, the curve will show you that this portfolio has a 90 percent chance of having an annual return for the next five years ranging from 2 percent per annum to 14 percent per annum, while the most likely return, the 50 percent line at the fattest part of the curve, shows an annualized return of 8 percent over five years.

Of course, as we discussed earlier, the longer the time span, the more likely the chances that your average return will be achieved. (Remember the example of the coin flip. If you flip a coin ten times, it might come up five tails and five heads, but it also might come up ten heads or ten tails. Only after you've done this millions of times will the result be very close to fifty-fifty.) The range of annual returns shrinks over the years. Remember the discussion of the one-year loss of 40 percent, as happened in 2008? Over a fifty-year period, that 40 percent one-year decline would barely move the needle on the long-term return of 8 percent.

FIGURE 3

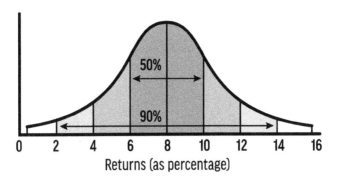

Source: Lynx Investment Advisory.

What's Wrong with This Picture?

The problem with the Gaussian bell curve, among other things, is that it does not accurately reflect "tail risk." So let's talk about tail risk. Notice how the tails of the curve slope down from the mean in a beautifully symmetrical shape. The point made by Mandelbrot, Taleb, and others who follow fractal geometry is that the perfectly symmetrical shape of the curve is an illusion, not a reality. In the real world, the roughness of the curve, and the roughness of life, means that unpredictable events will occur, and by definition they will be events we cannot anticipate. And here is the key point: *these events will occur more frequently than the bell curve analysis suggests, and the events will be far larger and more damaging.* In other words, the tails are generally fatter than the bell curve suggests. Look again at the bell curve below (figure 4):

FIGURE 4

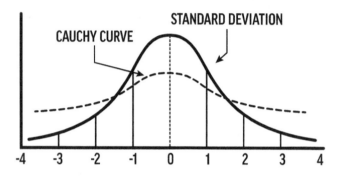

Source: Lynx Investment Advisory.

Another great French mathematician, Augustin Louis Cauchy (1789–1857), may well have understood probability better than Harry Markowitz or any of his predecessors. (Indeed, the French are not only good at making fine wine, foie gras, and champagne; they have excelled in math.) Cauchy launched the theory of functions of a complex variable, and don't worry if you don't know what that means. The mathematicians will know. More important to us is what Cauchy had to say about probability and its application to standard deviation.

Look at figure 4. We have used a dotted line to indicate a curve technically known as a Cauchy curve along with the Gaussian bell curve, which you are already familiar with. Although both curves look similar, the difference between Cauchy and Gaussian is very fundamental. Note that the Gaussian curve falls off very rapidly as you get away from the central region, whereas the Cauchy curve has fat, extended "tails." Technically, the curve is also known as a special case of "Student's t-distribution" with a degree of freedom of one. Because the decrease to infinity is slow, the Cauchy distribution has no mean and therefore no standard deviation, and it is outside the realm of the Central Limit Theorem. The importance of this to our discussion is that the Cauchy curve clearly indicates that the "tail," or rare events, are more likely than suggested by the Gaussian bell curve. However, if you ask Nassim Nicholas Taleb, he'll tell you that "fat tails" are not necessarily an indication of increased frequency. Instead, the "fat tails" tell us that the frequency of these events might actually be *less* than normal, but their effect is dramatically more explosive.

Think about the financial meltdown and the crash of 2008–2009 in this context.

The aforementioned Taleb's *The Black Swan* is one of the most important books ever written about risk. As defined by Taleb, "a Black Swan event comes from our misunderstanding of the likelihood of surprises because we take what we know a little too seriously." The point about the Black Swan is that it is an event that cannot be predicted. Again, as Taleb points out, "if you know that the stock market *can* crash, as it did in 1987, then such an event is not a Black Swan." Events that we can somehow take into account, like earthquakes and stock market crashes, are defined by Taleb as "Mandelbrotian Gray Swans." An example of a Black Swan event is the terrorist attack on 9/11. Again, Taleb notes, "Had the risk been reasonably conceivable … fighter planes would have circled the sky above the twin towers, airplanes would have had locked bulletproof doors, and the attack would not have taken place, period."

Imagine, then, that the Gaussian bell curve, a major pillar of Modern Portfolio Theory, may be very, very wrong in estimating our risk in the stock market. Oh, Freddie Gauss, have you misled us? I'm in good company here in criticizing Friedrich Gauss and his bell curve. Taleb describes the Gaussian bell curve as "a contagious and severe delusion." Right on.

Let's look at some specific examples of rare events and their odds according to the bell curve. In his book *The (Mis)behavior of Markets*, Mandelbrot cites a 2002 Citigroup study on currency price swings.[4]

In one day, the dollar rose against the Japanese yen by 3.78 percent, which is five standard deviations from the average. On the Gaussian bell curve, this would happen only once in a century. In the same study, the biggest currency decline of the yen versus the dollar was 7.9 percent.

The odds of that happening, based on the bell curve and standard deviation? Oh, about once every fifteen billion years!

Here are some other examples to ponder. In August 1998, a number of unpleasant occurrences caused a near panic in the stock and currency markets. The US president was fighting an impeachment by Congress, the Chinese were

---

4   Benoit Mandelbrot and Richard L Hudson, *The (Mis)behavior of Markets: A Fractal View of Financial Turbulence* (Basic Books, Mar 22, 2007).

rumored to be considering a devaluation of their currency, and Russia was enduring a cash squeeze and nearing default on its bonds. The combination of these problems caused rising discomfort on Wall Street, and the stock market reacted predictably and swiftly. On August 4, 1998, the Dow Jones Industrial Average declined 3.5 percent. But the final crushing blow came on the last day of the month, August 31, when the market tumbled a dizzying 6.8 percent, a bona fide meltdown.

Back to our Modern Portfolio Theory probability. What are the chances of a one-day decline in the US stock market of 6.8 percent? One in twenty million. If you were a daily stock trader, you would not expect to see such an occurrence in one hundred thousand years of trading. And the odds of getting three daily declines of over 3.5 percent in a single month, which happened in August 1998, is about one in five hundred *billion*.

Rare indeed. Or was it? Mandelbrot points out that in 1997, the Dow had fallen 7.7 percent in a single day. The odds of that happening are one in fifty billion. And of course, there was the crash of October 19, 1987, when the market, as measured by the Dow Jones Industrial Average, tumbled an incredible almost 22.6 percent. The odds of that happening are virtually incalculable. There is no number for that probability that would have any meaning.

How about some more recent examples? On October 15, 2008, the Dow tumbled by 7.87 percent. The probability of that happening, using the bell curve analysis, is one in fifty billion. So after that traumatic day, you were safe for another fifty billion years or so, right? Maybe not. Just forty-five days later, on December 1, 2008, the market, as measured by the Dow, again fell 7.7 percent. At the risk of beating this point to death, we want to make this very clear to you. So let's look back at the history of the stock market and see if the bell curve probability stood the test of time. We mentioned a few paragraphs back that according to the Gaussian bell curve, the odds of three daily stock market declines of 3.5 percent or more in a single month are about one in five hundred billion. (Yes, *billion*.) If that's true, we would be lucky, or unlucky, to encounter such a month once in a lifetime. Well, let's look back at the Dow Jones Industrial Average, which has a record back to 1928. Now let's count the number of times there was a daily decline of 3.5 percent or more in a single month. How many would you guess? One … maybe two? We counted twenty-six months in which there were three or more daily declines of 3.5 percent or more in a month since 1928! Does a single occurrence like that sound like a one-in-five-hundred-million probability?

One final example: We cited earlier that the chance of a 6.8 percent one-day decline in the bell curve in the US stock market was one in twenty million. A daily stock trader would not expect to see such an occurrence if he traded for one hundred thousand years. Here's the reality check: since 1928, there have been twenty-five instances of the Dow Jones Average losing 6.8 percent or more in a single day.

No wonder investment advisors are spooked about risk! Remember, your investment advisor really cares about you and wants to ensure that both your investment portfolio and your mental health are in good shape. The market shocks that I just described are far more frequent than the Gaussian bell curve would suggest, and that can cause far more frequent heartburn for you and your advisor. This will cause the investment advisor to double down on protecting your portfolio from decline, which has the effect of greatly reducing your long-term upside earning potential.

The takeaway point is that this higher-than-expected frequency of calamitous financial events seems to contradict the point made in chapter 5 that stock market declines of more than 40 percent are rarer than most people think. What Taleb and Mandelbrot are saying is that the frequency of short-term declines is far greater than the symmetrical Gaussian bell curve would indicate. In the case of major stock market declines, we are looking at peak-to-trough declines of 40 percent or greater over a period of time, and these are rare indeed. And that is precisely why you need to ignore these temporary market declines and stay invested to grow your multimillion-dollar retirement fund.

Are You Getting the Picture Now?

If a one-in-fifty-billion-chance event occurs, then a similar event happens soon after, what would you think about this succession of highly improbable events happening at regular intervals? We can think of only one answer: *The odds are wrong!* Mandelbrot's (and Taleb's) point is that the Gaussian bell curve and its neatly defined probability statistics do not represent the reality of how often tumultuous and tragic events really do occur. Mandelbrot's fractal geometry tells us that the world is not a smooth, orderly place. Reality is tinged with roughness. Here's a simple example: When a child draws a mountain, a cloud, or a Christmas tree, what does it look like? We easily imagine the straight lines and smooth curves of these drawings. But we also know that this is not what they really look like! In Mandelbrot's own words,

> Risk is also not symmetrical, the bell curve is not accurate about risk, and catastrophic events like market crashes occur far more often than the investment community has assumed.

Clouds are not spheres, mountains are not cones, coastlines are not circles, and bark is not smooth, nor does lightning travel in a straight line.[5]

Risk is also not symmetrical, the bell curve is not accurate about risk, and catastrophic events like market crashes occur far more often than the

---

5   B. B. Mandelbrot, *The Fractal Geometry of Nature* (San Francisco: W. H. Freeman, 1982.)

investment community has assumed based on the theories that have guided the industry for a long time. And remember, risk does not always result in tragedy. Risk is sometimes rewarded. In 2009, the stock market had a violent and swift recovery from its lows in March, rising over 50 percent by the end of summer.

In short, we thought we understood risk, but we didn't.

Here's why this is important. We invest in a portfolio of stocks because we expect our investments to grow over the years and increase our fortunes. Most of the time, for prudent and savvy investors, that will happen. For others, it won't, and the losses may well be catastrophic. The losers will be the ones who do not have a long-term investing objective and who panic out of stocks at the wrong time. That is precisely what the investment professionals fear most, and that is precisely why they want you to stuff your portfolio with noncorrelating (does that rhyme with *nonperforming*?) asset classes to lower your short-term risk of loss at the expense of your long-term prospect for a high return. With a new and deeper understanding of the risks in investing, your multimillion-dollar portfolio will achieve your expected return as long as you are convinced that scary short-term market events will not disrupt your long-term investment success.

The first lesson of the recent past is that we must be prepared for cataclysmic market declines that will occur more than once every few billion years. Indeed, investors were blindsided by the horrendous asset price declines in 2008 and 2009. Those who panicked and sold out were mistaken, and they will not retire with multimillion-dollar portfolios.

To be clear, Mandelbrot's contribution to our understanding of risk is highly important in that it debunks the neat and symmetric distributions and probability of the bell curve when it comes to the frequency of calamitous financial market events. But what Mandelbrot's work *does not do* is tell us when or how frequently these catastrophic events will occur. It does not provide a road map we can follow with a person ready to wave a red flag when necessary: "Watch out! Danger ahead!" Instead, his work cautions us not to rely on the old theories of probability.

This is why so many investors and their advisors are afraid to take the risk of recommending a portfolio with high equity content.

We have learned that market crashes can be severe and, although rare, are not as infrequent as older analyses might have projected.

Conclusion: Modern Portfolio Theory, with its bell curve and asset allocation, has many useful features. Markowitz's contribution to our knowledge of investing is firmly implanted and will remain an important addition to investment theory and practice. But the part of the theory that involves the bell curve is *wrong* when it comes to the probability estimates of the standard bell curve. If we have learned anything from recent market collapses, it is this: turbulent, even catastrophic, markets will occur *far more frequently* than we originally thought. Similarly, positive market surprises will also occur. Risk works both ways.

> *But the fear of a market collapse should not overshadow the fact that over the long term, the stock market will continue to make new highs, as it has for a century.*

Our challenge can be simply stated. We need to position ourselves to profit from upside risk that is rewarded and not dread dramatic stock market downturns that will come more frequently than we might have expected in the past. As you save for retirement, do not make the mistake of tailoring your portfolio based on fear; market crashes will occur, but your path to a multimillion-dollar retirement involves investing exclusively, or nearly exclusively, in the stock market over two decades or longer. There are no two-decade periods in stock market history where money was lost. Please read this last sentence again.

CHAPTER SEVEN

To Get Rich, Buy Stocks. But How?

As you know by now, the principal lesson in this book is that in order to become rich by investing, you must buy stocks. Everyone knows this, but how do we go about it? There are a number of options.

Pick and Choose

Some investors like the idea of doing research and picking stocks themselves. Some are actually quite good at it, but to be honest, the good ones are few and far between.

If you are tempted to build your fortune by picking stocks yourself, before you get started, please answer this question: Assuming you are not a professional investor and spend limited time researching the stock market, how do you plan to do better than a professional fund manager who spends forty hours a week doing this exact job? I haven't found a good answer to that question yet, with the exception of the amateur investor who succeeds by luck. And guess what? Even professional investors don't usually beat stock market performance. If you have read any of my previous investment books, you will recognize this exact question, because I hammer it home every chance I get. No one has yet been able to explain to me how they are going to beat the performance of a pro who spends all day researching investments while you, the enlightened amateur, spend only a fraction of that amount of time doing the same thing. My advice: Do not pick and choose stocks yourself.

Buy a Mutual Fund

Let's agree that for long-term retirement accounts, we should leave the investing chores to the professionals. That will lead us to consider investing in a mutual fund or an exchange-traded fund (ETF). A mutual fund is a pool of money invested in the stock market, or in a sector of the stock market such as small-capitalization ("cap") stocks, large-cap stocks, value stocks, growth stocks, international stocks, and the list goes on. An ETF is also a fund, but similar to stocks, ETFs trade on the stock exchange. In the case of most mutual funds, you can only buy shares once a day after the market closes. Mutual funds are professionally managed by one or more portfolio managers, priced at the end of each day, with the share price based on the performance of the stocks owned by the mutual fund. These funds are generally "open ended," which means that anyone can buy or sell shares in the fund, and the total value of the fund is a function of how much money flows into or out of the fund. Some mutual funds are very large, with billions of dollars invested in them by thousands of investors. Others are smaller.

Once you buy a mutual fund, you will naturally be interested in how well the fund is performing. Most funds have a benchmark, which is a barometer of how well the fund is doing. In general, a large-cap fund will be benchmarked against a large-cap index, such as the S&P 500

Index, which is an index based on the value of the five hundred largest companies listed on the various stock exchanges. You can actually own the S&P 500 value by buying what is known as an index fund. Mutual funds that are invested in large-company stocks try to beat the performance of the S&P Index because it's known that investors always have a choice of investing in a mutual fund or an index fund.

Active versus Passive

There is an eternal debate in the investment industry about the merits of active versus passive investing. Here's what it means. Passive investing is the practical application of the Efficient Market Theory (EMT), which is the investing approach that says that it is so hard to beat the market that you shouldn't even bother trying. The stock market is efficient; everything that is public information about any stock is instantly reflected in that stock's price. Thus goes the Efficient Market Theory. So if there is no information advantage, anyone who invests doesn't know any more about a company's future than anyone else. If you pick stocks based on some theory that the stock price is going to rise, if it does rise, the EMT folks will claim you were just lucky. Why? Because you had no way of knowing any more about the company than anyone else who studied all the publicly available information about that company's stock. Anyway, that's the theory.

Do you believe it?

Hold your judgment for a bit longer while we go on.

Funds that are managed by a fund manager are referred to as actively managed funds. An S&P 500 Index fund, which really isn't managed since it simply owns the top five hundred companies, is referred to as a passive fund, or an index fund. Keep in mind that there are many widely used indexes. There are small-cap stock indexes, midcap stock indexes, international indexes, and even indexes by types of stock. Mutual fund managers should be benchmarked and evaluated by comparing their performance to the performance of an index that is invested similarly. So if you pick a mutual fund that only invests in small-company stocks, it would be neither fair nor accurate to compare the performance of that fund against the performance of a fund that only invests in large-company stocks. In order to get an apples-to-apples correct performance comparison, a small-cap mutual fund should not be measured against the S&P 500 Index, which is an index of large companies. A small-cap fund should instead be compared to the performance of a small-cap index, such as the Russell 2000, which includes two thousand smaller companies. Apples to apples.

These performance comparisons are important because stocks, like cattle, tend to move in herds, depending on the stock market moods and preferences at any given time. There are times when the market hates large-company stocks but loves small-company stocks, and vice versa. So it's important to compare performance of any fund to the benchmark that is most like it in its investment philosophy and practice.

Pick a Style

Next is the question of style. The two types of investment styles are value and growth. The value investor is essentially a bargain hunter, someone who shops at outlet malls and looks for the best deals available. Stocks of this sort are generally stocks in companies that are down on their luck and might have suffered a setback or two, and as a result, the stock trades at a very low price. The value investor is looking to buy the stock cheap, when its price has been whacked, and then wait for a recovery. Of course, the recovery might or might not happen, so this is where good analysis becomes an important factor.

Growth investors are the opposite of value investors. They are not looking for bargains; they are looking for growth. They want to buy companies that are growing rapidly in both revenue and earnings, even if the stock price has been bid up by other enthusiastic buyers looking for the same thing. Growth investors are betting that the growth will continue and the price will keep going up. The risk here is that if for whatever reason the growth slows or even stops, investors will be disappointed and sell their shares, and the stock will plummet. In addition to ensuring that we compare our fund performance to the right benchmark by size, we must also make sure that we compare the fund performance to the right style of benchmark too.

Which Funds Should You Pick?

The first decision you must make is whether to go active or passive. This means that you need to decide whether you will buy a fund managed by professional managers or just settle on an index fund that mirrors the performance of the stock market or a segment of the market (such as small-cap stocks, tech stocks, healthcare stocks, etc.). I am going to try to make this choice easy for you.

First, let's consider the question of fees. Active funds are managed by real people who are seasoned market professionals, trained in the intricacies of finance. These folks are also a group of well-paid men and women, young and old. Active funds charge a fee to cover the cost of paying all these people, plus marketing costs, research costs, rent, and so forth. Fund fees vary, but an average annual fee might be 1 percent of the amount invested, which means that for every one hundred dollars you invest in that fund, ninety-nine goes to your investment in year one, and one dollar pays the cost of managing the fund. It doesn't sound like much, but fees can take a significant chunk out of your results over time. The question becomes,

Are you getting enough return to justify the fund fees you are paying? This question is important, because if you buy an index fund, the fee you pay is much lower. That's because index funds do not require a great deal of management or decision-making. All the index fund has to do is buy the same stocks that are in the index that you might otherwise be trying to beat. In most cases, the preferred index will be the S&P 500, which will give you a broad representation of the stock market behavior through the performance of the five hundred largest companies on the market. The fee will be a fraction of the fees charged by active managers. In many cases, the index fund fee might be 0.1 percent of the fund value, which is about one-tenth the fee of many actively managed funds.

A Very Brief Primer on the Efficient Market Theory

The Efficient Market Theory is likely the most discussed, argued about, and long-lasting topic of debate in the investment industry. Countless books have been written about it, including one of mine, *Investment Gurus*, which features interviews with well-known investment management stars like Peter Lynch and Mario Gabelli matched against finance academics, three of whom won the Nobel Prize in economics. As I mentioned earlier, the Efficient Market Theory holds that everything that is publicly known about any company is instantly reflected in the price of that company's stock.

Almost all finance academics believe in this theory, and almost none of the active managers agree with them. The theory sounds simple enough, but the implications of the theory are huge. If you accept that a company's stock price reflects everything that can be known about the company at any given time, then you must accept that no one has any advantage over anyone else in determining how the stock will behave in the future. What that means is that anyone whose performance beats the stock market's performance can only do so by luck, since there is no information advantage. Let

> **The stock market is not perfectly and instantaneously efficient. Instead, it is constantly in the process of becoming efficient.**

me point out that after the many interviews I did for *Investment Gurus*, I concluded that the stock market is not perfectly and instantaneously efficient. Instead, it is constantly in the *process* of becoming efficient. For example, let's say that a company announces it has discovered a new technology that will help find a cure in a particular field of cancer research. I believe that this information will take time to get processed and that the effects of the discovery will not be instantly reflected in the company's stock price. How many individuals will be affected by this discovery? How unique is it? Are other companies also poised to find a cure? And many other questions will take time to sort out. If someone is clever enough to ask the right questions and get positive answers, that person can buy the stock before others discover the good news and thus create an advantage through good research.

The significant issue with the Efficient Market Theory is that if you believe in it, then you must conclude that great managers like Peter Lynch, Warren Buffett, Mario Gabelli, George Soros, and the like got rich by luck, not because they were smarter than everyone else. Try telling them that.

Once Again, Active versus Passive

What is the best way to help you decide whether to buy an active versus passive fund, or index fund? Simple. If I pay a fee to an active manager who runs a mutual fund, then she must justify the fee I pay her by beating her benchmark, which is the index fund I might have bought instead. If she invests in large-company stocks, I want to benchmark her performance against the performance of the S&P 500 Index. In order to justify the higher fee I am paying her to actively manage her fund, she must give me a better return over time than I would get by simply buying the index and paying a much lower fee. I mention "over time" because I can't realistically expect my fund manager to beat the index every year. But over a multiyear period, she needs to beat the index if she wants me to stay invested in her fund.

The question then arises, Is it hard for a talented fund manager to beat the index? The answer: very hard.

The Evidence

Over the years, studies have been conducted to compare the performance of actively managed funds versus the S&P 500 Index. In most cases, the indexes won.

In 2019, Bob Pisani of CNBC reported that in 2018, the S&P 500 outperformed 64.5 percent of large-cap actively managed funds.[6]

We'll agree that a one-year performance doesn't tell us very much, whereas a longer-term comparison will offer a more statistically useful correlation. It turns out that Standard & Poor's performs the study every year. For the ten years that ended in 2018, the S&P 500 Index beat 85 percent of active fund managers. It gets worse. For the fifteen-year period, the index beat 91.6 percent of active managers. Here's another important factor based on my own investigation into the performance comparison derby. Of those few managers who beat the index over a long period of time, the majority of them did so by such a small

---

6   Bob Pisani, "TRADER TALK: Active fund managers trail the S&P 500 for the ninth year in a row in triumph for indexing," CNBC, March 15, 2019, https://www.cnbc.com/2019/03/15/active-fund-managers-trail-the-sp-500-for-the-ninth-year-in-a-row-in-triumph-for-indexing.html.

margin that it would have made little difference in the overall outcome in your portfolio. Another nail in the coffin of active management. As we pointed out, this study involves large-cap fund managers who are properly benchmarked against the S&P 500 Index. Interestingly, the study was also performed on other types of active managers, like small-cap and even bond managers. Overall, roughly 80 percent of all types of active managers underperformed their indexes.

These results give finance academics the opportunity to nod knowingly and convey with a wry smile that their Efficient Market Theory is correct. It is very difficult to beat the index, and if you do, it is more likely that you won by luck, not skill. Their theory is reinforced by what is called persistence. They will point out that when funds do beat the index, they don't do it for very long. Yes, there are exceptions. Peter Lynch's performance always comes to mind, along with a few others who have enjoyed great performance over many years. However, the exceptions are few and far between. Very few funds consistently beat the market. That fact adds credibility to the Efficient Market Theory. As I mentioned, there are some persistent winners. Warren Buffett has been doing it for decades,

George Soros has an extraordinary record, and a handful of hedge fund managers became billionaires by providing superior long-term investment performance. The academics will point out that when we talk of consistently superior performance, we keep repeating the same handful of names. These are the exceptions, they say.

Conclusion

The investment plan in this book involves making a fortune in the stock market over several decades. History shows that if you decide to pick one or more actively managed funds as part of your investment plan, your chances of success are only about one in ten. Moreover, even if you are lucky enough to pick the few winners, the majority of those who beat the index did so by small margins. In the end, you would need to pick one of a small group of managers who beat the market by a big enough margin to make a difference in your overall performance. That raises the odds of doing so, shifting it closer to one in thirty. It becomes clear that investing in index funds is the best solution to capture the long-term returns of the stock market with a minimum of risk.

CHAPTER EIGHT

The Pure Equity Plus Plan, Part One: A Look at History

H ere are the takeaways from this book so far: first, the stock market can be very volatile, with potential declines as much as 40 percent or greater, but these don't happen very often. Second, the path to great wealth in the stock market is not bonds, not cash, not diversification, not asset allocation, just one thing: stocks. Achieving your goal of wealth will require conviction and discipline. We're going to help make that feasible.

In previous chapters, we focused our attention on the major declines in stock prices occurring over the years. The investment industry has built its entire business on confronting those declines from a *psychological* point of view, not an *investment* point of view. History shows that over time the market always goes up, but those in-between periods can be long and frustrating. Consider the following two examples.

Great Decades to Own Stocks

In the decade beginning August 1990 and ending August 2000, the total ten-year gain was 493 percent, or an annualized gain of 19.5 percent, with dividends reinvested. And how much work did you put in to get these sensational returns? Pretty much none. Oh yes, ten years earlier you made a decision to invest in the S&P 500 Index, then you forgot about it. These gains assume you put a lump sum of money in the index and locked it up for ten years. More realistically, think about how much more you'd have earned if you'd invested every month out of your paycheck, adding to your fortune gradually using a payroll deduction plan. Later in the book, we'll show you how much money a systematic savings plan might generate.

So much for a great return decade.

A Terrible Decade to Own Stocks

Now let's look at an example of a bad decade. If you had invested in the S&P 500 Index from February 1999 to February 2009, your decade-long investment would have resulted not in a gain but in a total loss of 29 percent, which is a loss of 3.4 percent on average each year. This is a perfect example of why the only winning strategy is investing for not one decade but for two or more decades. Taking the same starting date of February 1999 and extending it for twenty years instead of ten, to February 2019, your market return, as measured by S&P 500 returns, would have been a cumulative return of 229.6 percent, or around 6 percent each year. That result would not have frightened you at all. But to get there, it was important for you to not give up in 2009, when you had a ten-year loss. This is why we recommend that you look at your long-term retirement account no more than once a year! If you are a Nervous Nellie and inclined to panic when stocks go down, honestly, you shouldn't invest in stocks at all.

It's all about time. Nothing but time.

I want to address a point that some might raise, with legitimate concerns. When you see various statistics describing the performance of the stock market over periods of time, you often encounter different results for the same periods. How can that be? For example, in one text, you might read that over a particular decade, the stock market rose 12 percent a year, while in another write-up, you find a statement that the market rose 10.8 percent over the exact same period! (I'm making up these numbers for the purposes of this example.) As it turns out, both numbers may be correct, and the difference is in how the returns were calculated. The simplest difference is likely to be in the frequency of the compounding of returns given that many stocks pay dividends that are then reinvested. As you'll see later on, we use monthly compounding of returns in our data rather than annual compounding, since by calculating the returns monthly, we get a more accurate return than by doing it only once a year. Also, in some cases, index returns are used without taking into account the dividends paid by the stocks in the index. Obviously, this will lead to a very different result when compared against statistics that take into account not just the index, but the dividends as well.

Another perplexing variable when calculating stock market returns is the issue of highs and lows. In some cases, stock market highs are calculated based on the *intraday* high, while in other cases, the *closing* high is used. Same for the lows. I point this out since as you read different sources of statistics, you may encounter differences in the numbers and wonder which is right. Often, they are both right, and you just need to know what basis of comparison was used. Confusing, isn't it?

Understanding Why PEPP Is the Best Opportunity to Retire with a Fortune

Not everyone who reads this book will start off with the same amount of money to invest, nor with the same amount to salt away every month. It is also true that each reader will have his or her own time period until retirement. For these reasons, we will prepare two levels of starting investments and monthly contributions. Your personal plan will either fit on one of these benchmarks or somewhere in between. Likewise, your time horizon will be a function of your starting date and the age at which you plan to retire.

When considering investment advice, we have all read countless times that past performance does not guarantee future results. The SEC requires investment advisors and brokers who list their past performance to add words to this effect, and for good reason, because we all know that no one can predict the future. Given that, how can I be so certain that you will get the results I believe you will get? It's pretty simple.

As is the case with the famous SEC legend, there are no guarantees here. The PEPP advantage is simply that we have a very long history of performance on our side. A hedge fund, money manager, or mutual fund might have a few sterling years of excellent performance, but that is no indication that the superior performance will continue. Yet the longer the sample period, the higher the confidence that the streak is genuine. For example, if I show you a five-year performance record by a mutual fund of, say, 15 percent a year, how confident are you that this wonderful performance will continue? I would not be confident at all, and neither should you. Why? Because over that five-year period, we don't really know if the manager was imbued with

The longer the sample period, the higher the confidence that the streak is genuine.

unusual and extraordinary talent, or if he was just lucky. But what if the performance record I showed you was not five, ten, or even twenty years long, but rather sixty years or longer? Might your confidence in that performance record be higher? Of course it would.

The PEPP investment portfolio I propose for you has that type of long performance history.

In order to put the right perspective on the performance of the stock market, let's have a look at the best and worst periods in stocks going back to 1957, when the S&P 500 Index was born. (These calculations involve dividends being reinvested, and for the period during which dividends were not segregated out from the index, data from the NYU Stern School of Business was used.)

BEST RETURNS			
	Cumulative	Annualized	Period
5 Years	271.66%	30.03%	07/30/82-07/31/87
10 Years	493.38%	19.49%	08/31/90-08/31/00
20 Years	2822.25%	18.38%	03/31/80-03/31/00

	WORST RETURNS		
	Cumulative	Annualized	Period
5 Years	-29.05%	-6.63%	02/27/04-02/27/09
10 Years	-29.48%	-3.43%	02/26/99-02/27/09
20 Years	154.83%	4.79%	03/31/00-03/31/20

Charts: Lynx Investment Advisory

As you can see, the best five-, ten-, and twenty-year performances for the stock market speak for themselves. No one is complaining. That's why we want to focus on the worst periods, since that will frame our understanding of how bad our investments could get, using a very long history as a guide. In fact, there are no twenty-year losses in history going back to World War II.

Dear friends, this may be the most important part of this book and the most important message we have to impart. Here's why: in order for you to make the decision you need to make to maximize your retirement gains, you must have the confidence that the higher volatility you may endure will pay off handsomely in the end. No, we can't predict the future, so history is our guide.

And history provides a solid degree of comfort. Please remember that.

CHAPTER NINE

The Pure Equity Plus Plan, Part Two: What the Future Holds

In this chapter, we begin to introduce the exact portfolio we recommend for your long-term retirement plan. This specific portfolio is the one that history suggests offers the best chance to make a large sum of money that will fuel your rich retirement. It is a simple portfolio, one you can rebalance every year, either by yourself or with the help of your advisor.

First, let's explain the elements of the portfolio so that you understand what they are and why they will be part of your investment plan.

In chapter 7, we went into detail about why it makes sense to invest passively in the stock market. From there we learned why it's important to buy the index to get the full stock market performance instead of taking a chance on picking one or more funds that hope to beat the stock market's performance. As the data shows, the vast majority of mutual funds and money managers do not beat the market averages, and my studies indicate that the few who do outperform beat the market by a very small margin that would not have a significant effect on your overall returns. Finally, there is the matter of fees. Mutual funds charge management fees of around 1 percent, so to beat the market they would first need to make up the 1 percent fee they charge you and *then* try to beat the market. An index fund costs around 0.1 percent, or about one-tenth the cost of an actively managed fund, so *we* get that fee advantage too. Given these facts, let's play it safe and stick with the index funds.

There is one additional and important fact you need to consider when picking a mutual fund. This is a point that few investors know about or even consider when buying an index fund.

The typical S&P 500 Index fund you buy is what is called "cap weighted." *Cap* stands for "capitalization." This means that the fund is weighted by the size of the companies that comprise the five hundred companies in the index. In turn, that means that company number five hundred in the index is much smaller than company number one, so the larger companies carry more weight in the index, and their price performance influences the index's price much more than smaller companies do.

Here's an example: In August 2020, the ten largest stocks in the S&P 500 Index accounted for 29 percent of the value of the index. Stocks of companies like Apple, Facebook, Alphabet Inc. (Google), Amazon, Microsoft, and Berkshire Hathaway were the largest part of this exclusive list. Think about this for a moment. Ten companies in an index composed of five hundred companies accounted for nearly one-third of the value of the index. So does the S&P 500 Index accurately represent the movement of the stock market, as represented by the five hundred companies that comprise the index? Well, no. Because the top ten stocks are going to have a hugely disproportionate effect on the price of the index. Apple alone represents about 7 percent of the index. What's more, note that the vast majority of these top ten companies are in the tech field. So any major event affecting stocks in the tech industry has a disproportionately large effect on the index. The bottom line is that the S&P 500 Index does not, in fact, provide exposure to the market as a whole, since it is immensely influenced by a handful of very large companies stemming from one industry.

What about the Dow Jones Industrial Average? Since it is the oldest index of the US stock market, going back to 1896, this index is primarily historical. With that said, it consists of only thirty stocks, so it is hardly representative of a market of thousands of companies.

The S&P 500 Index, with its faults, remains the leading, most comprehensive stock market index we use. But there is an alternative.

In addition to the S&P 500 Index, which is capitalization weighted, there are indexes of the very same type that are calculated differently. Instead of calculating the index by market capitalization of its component companies, the equal-weighted index gives each of the five hundred companies the exact same weight. This eliminates the problem of having a handful of companies exercising an undue influence on the value of the index. The equal-weighted index gives a much truer picture of the market as a whole.

Now comes the $64,000 question: Which index is better, the cap-weighted or the equal-weighted S&P 500? See the graph below, and judge for yourself.

FIGURE 5

S&P 500 TR vs S&P 500 Equal Weight TR (base 100 on December 29, 1989)

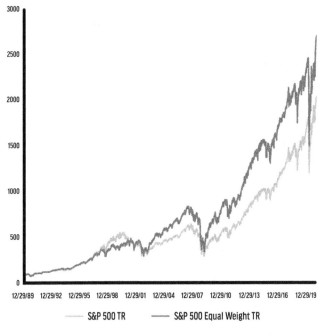

Chart by Peter Pavlov, Lynx Investment Advisory

As we just observed, the equal-weighted index has outperformed the cap-weighted version, which demands that we should pay attention. In the portfolio we suggest for you, we recommend using both. This is because the two index configurations behave differently, and the combination of their performances can serve us well, since we cannot predict when the outperformance of one over the other will occur. In the example used earlier, where ten companies in the index accounted for nearly a third of the value of the entire five hundred, that happened because those high-flying tech stocks were on a tear, and their rapid rise propelled the entire index. Yes, we'd like to be part of that. But should the market turn in the other direction and start to plummet, having the equal-weighted index in our portfolio will stabilize the roller-coaster ride.

Gold

A depiction of the French Louis d'or

Allow me to begin this discussion with a very personal anecdote. In the late 1960s, I lived with my young family in Paris, where I was the manager of the Smith, Barney investment office. The year 1968 brought events in France that would go down in history. History buffs, and all Frenchmen who were alive then, remember the frightening sequence of events that occurred in May of that year. A series of strikes and labor actions, followed by a student revolt, brought the country to a complete stand-still. First the Metro and bus lines went on strike, then train service came to a halt. Soon the airports ceased to function, and there was no longer a supply of gasoline with which to fill your car's gas tank, which at that point was the only remaining means of escape. Riots in the Latin Quarter of Paris challenged the police as cars were overturned and burned. The country had reached a boiling point. The American embassy prepared evacuation plans for American citizens, but even those plans were problematic given that no transportation facilities in the country were operational. France's president, General Charles de Gaulle of World War II fame, was nowhere to be found.

As a young family with two small children, to say that we were frightened is an understatement. We decided to do whatever we could to get out of Paris. I had a car with a full tank of gas, and we planned to head south, to the Italian border. Of course, one tank of gas wouldn't get us that far, so we hoped that somewhere near the city of Lyon, we might be able to find gas. But how to pay for it?

In many societies, including our own, families keep a nest egg for emergencies. Some hide cash in the proverbial mattress or hang on to Treasury bonds. In France, the older families almost universally hold a stash of gold, and it is almost always in the form of Louis d'ors. These are gold coins first introduced by King Louis XIII in 1640. The name derives from the depiction of King Louis on one side of the coin and the French royal coat of arms on the reverse. The French know value when they see it, and in a time of extreme crisis, paper currency may have limited value. Gold's value, they believe, is universal.

As my family packed and prepared to leave Paris in our Peugeot 404, one of my colleagues at work handed me two Louis d'ors. "Here," he said. "If you need gas or anything else, this may be the only currency they will accept." I accepted the coins graciously, and we departed.

The end of this story is that we made it to the south of France and decided to stay there as the crisis began to ebb. By the time we returned to Paris several weeks later, the crisis had ended. But it is a crisis the French will never forget, and neither will we.

As a footnote to this anecdote, I am compelled to add that many years later, while living in Washington, where I now reside, I was at a reception and was chatting with the French ambassador to the US. He asked me about my time living in Paris, and I told him the story I just related above. I explained to him how frightened we were at the sight of the enraged students throwing rocks at the police and burning cars. The ambassador smiled at me and said, "My dear friend, I was one of those students protesting and throwing rocks!" Times change.

I recount this story as an introduction to this recommendation for your Pure Equity Plus portfolio. In addition to your investment in the two S&P 500 indexes, your portfolio will have a small amount of one additional element: gold. The gold in your retirement portfolio is just a bit of insurance against extreme events, what Nassim Taleb popularized in his book *The Black Swan*, a perennial best seller that has transformed the way we look at risk. The phrase *Black Swan* refers to those highly improbable events that strike when least expected. The 2008–2009 financial meltdown that we described earlier was such an event.

The effect of Black Swans is that they can cause severe damage to your portfolio, not to mention your psychological well-being. When extreme uncertainty unfolds, gold shines. Gold is also a protection against severe inflation, something we haven't experienced in the US since the 1970s. Could it come back? Yes. And it might. The astronomical federal budget deficits we are experiencing, which were already bad and are now exacerbated by the COVID-19 pandemic, may one day hit us hard by causing interest rates to rise, perhaps dramatically. So the gold will be there to mitigate the effect of any economic Black Swans that may come along. The idea is that the rise in gold during times of financial stress will mitigate the damage to the rest of the portfolio, however slightly, and will also give us a head start when the recovery comes.

When extreme uncertainty unfolds, gold shines.

Those who oppose owning gold sniff at the idea of holding it as an investment, stating that it does nothing productive. It has no earnings, pays no dividends, and doesn't contribute to the economy; it just sits there looking pretty. Yet no other investment has a history of demand like gold. Think about it this way. We speak today of long-term investments, like blue chip stocks of major companies that have been around for decades. Gold has a history that puts every other investment to shame. How many other investments can you think of that were mentioned in the Bible? Gold has appealed to us humans for thousands of years. In many countries, such as India, it is part of the culture. Every Indian wedding highlights gifts of gold. Given that gold is a precious commodity, it cannot be duplicated other than by finding a mine and digging it out. As mining techniques have improved over the centuries, we continue to discover more of the commodity, but it is clear that it will not be available indefinitely. The combination of gold's rarity and its beauty has attracted us forever.

Gold's universal desirability is such that throughout the ages it has been recognized as a secure store of value. Paper currency is just that—paper—and when confidence in a currency is shaken, the authorities keep adding zeros to their paper bills. Many of us have souvenir Zimbabwe bills in denominations of several trillion dollars. Yes, this is a real banknote:

FIGURE 6

Gold has a place in our future long-term investment plans, and that is why it is part of the Pure Equity Plus Plan.

The Lifetime Portfolio

The Pure Equity Plus Plan I recommend is simple and will guide you through a lifetime. You will invest your money as follows: 45 percent in an equal-weighted S&P 500 Index fund, 45 percent in a capitalization-weighted S&P 500 Index fund, and 10 percent in gold, by buying the gold ETF, GLD, or, if you prefer, gold coins for storage in a safe place. You can rest comfortably in the knowledge that your 90 percent investment in stocks has a performance record of almost one hundred years, and the actual S&P 500 Index performance goes back to 1957.

A Word about Backtests

A backtest is a test that demonstrates how a particular theory would have worked had it been used in the past—for example, if we develop a theory that shows you investing in stocks with names that start with the first ten letters of the alphabet in odd years, and in even years you invest in stocks that start with the last ten letters of the alphabet, this secret formula would guarantee your investment returns would far exceed a simple investment in the stock market averages. And what's more, we can prove it!

The problem with backtests is that by creating them after the fact, we can demonstrate some pretty amazing statistics about stock market returns. In fact, most twelve-year-olds can do this pretty convincingly. All you need to do is look for a pattern in the past that produces magical results and assume this pattern will continue into the future. Old-timers will remember the stock market pattern that seemed to coincide with the length of women's skirts. When skirt lengths rose, so did the stock market, and vice versa. Now, trying to figure out a logical reason why this might be required a great deal of imagination, and no one really tried. It just happened that way. But would that pattern continue? What do you think?

I bring this up now because in this book we are using a backtest to make our point. The recommended portfolio is the one that you can count on to succeed greatly in the stock market and retire rich. But if backtests are not reliable, why are we using one?

Backtests tend to be short-term phenomena, patterns that are randomly formed (women's hemlines, for example), and we apply these patterns to some other event, like rises and declines in stock prices. This becomes a problem of correlation versus causation. The data may correlate, but they don't cause events to happen. The hemline lengths of women's skirts don't really influence stock prices, even though it may look like they follow a similar magical pattern.

The backtest we are using has two features that make it unlike its dubious counterparts.

First, we are using data that goes back nearly one hundred years. Any pattern that stands that long a test of time achieves credibility by virtue of its endurance. Second, the proof of the very long backtest is explainable. The very long-term growth of stock prices in the US economy coincides with the growth of the US economy itself. Not all companies prosper, but the majority of companies that do prosper are the cause of economic growth. What's more, the US economy has gone through major changes in the way we live and in the way the economy changes accordingly. In 1900, the United States was an agricultural economy, where the majority of its working citizens were engaged in farming and businesses associated with producing food. The average life span was about fifty years. This was the era that followed the discovery of electricity and the start of the American Industrial Revolution. In the forties and fifties, America was the leading manufacturing economy in the world. As other countries learned to build things faster and cheaper, the US didn't fade away; we transitioned to what we are today: the preeminent knowledge economy in the world. In the 1950s, the biggest companies in the world were General Motors, General Electric, Exxon (then Standard

Oil Company [New Jersey]), Ford, and other manufacturing and energy behemoths. Today, the largest companies in the world are Facebook, Google, Amazon, and Apple, all companies that didn't exist a few decades ago. The premise of our investment plan is that the United States will continue to innovate, grow, and transform itself in the future, just as it has done over the past two hundred years. If there is an article of faith in investing, this is it: the US will continue to grow and excel. To the extent we use backtests, they are based on the principles of US exceptionalism and its corresponding growth.

CHAPTER TEN

What About International Diversification?

s any self-respecting investment advisor will tell you, the United States stock market isn't the only stock market in the world. Indeed, the capitalization of US stocks represents only about 55 percent of world stock market values. It seems to make sense that an investor should have some investments in the rest of the world besides the United States. What might we be missing by investing solely in US stocks?

The answer: not much.

Have a look at the chart below, which shows the returns of the major stock markets, some going back 120 years. You will quickly notice that the only stock market that beats the US over a very long period of time is Australia, and it wins by a very small margin. It's also helpful to know that the Australian stock market is only a fraction of the size of the US stock market. A quick look at this chart will explain why legendary investor Warren Buffett spends very little time looking for opportunities outside the US.

FIGURE 7

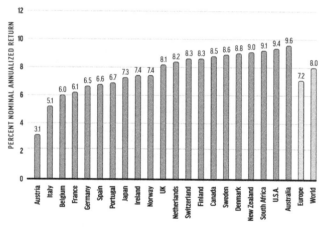

Nominal Annualized Return for Global Stocks from 1900 to 2019

Credit Suisse report prepared by Elroy Dimson, Cambridge University, and Paul Marsh and Mike Staunton, London Business School.

As you are most likely aware, the countries in the chart are mostly developed countries. Using the above graph, the annualized return for the stocks in these developed countries, including the US, over a very long period is 8 percent, a very fine result but nowhere near as good as the US performance of 9.4 percent. Now, although the chart purports to show returns going back to 1900, not all these countries have data going back that far. Given that we are comparing international markets to the US market, we'll want to know what the overseas market returns were *without* the US results. A different study (other than the Credit Suisse one) indicates that the returns (since 1986) for developed markets outside the US was 7.1 percent.

The evidence clearly suggests that over the long term, investment in the US stock market has been the most successful. By logical extension, that means that diversifying your portfolio internationally will more likely lower your long-term returns rather than enhance them, again over a long period of time.

> **Investment in the US stock market has been the most successful.**

However, diversification might benefit you by smoothing out the portfolio returns, given that history shows that US markets and international developed markets don't move in lockstep. Indeed, there are periods when American stock markets both outperformed and underperformed their overseas counterparts, hence smoothing out your yearly returns. But was your overall return higher by diversifying internationally? No.

Before we leave this discussion, let's have a look at emerging markets.

Does It Pay to Invest in Emerging Markets?

Emerging markets are stock markets in countries that have not yet achieved economic maturity and are generally growing at a rapid rate. They tend to lack the sophisticated institutional structures that developed markets enjoy, particularly in the area of the country's judiciary and in the regulations of stock markets. Examples of emerging markets include Egypt, Turkey, China, Vietnam, and many others.

Many advisors recommend that a portion of a well-diversified portfolio should be invested in emerging markets. Over long periods, emerging-market stocks have had a performance slightly higher than the US stock market, but at a cost of considerably higher volatility. Because this is likely the riskiest asset class that most portfolios will contain, the proposed allocation will generally be small. The case for the emerging markets allocation can be compelling, but it deserves further analysis. Proponents of this type of diversification are fond of pointing out a recent example of how emerging markets performed compared to the developed markets in a time of crisis.

As we have seen, a terrible decade for investments in stocks was the first decade of the new century, from 2000 to 2009. During that ten-year period, the US stock market had a slightly *negative* return, an amount of time that would try the patience of even the most patient investor. However, during that same period, emerging markets had an annualized return of 9.8 percent. Pretty amazing. The fellows who actively advocate diversification will eagerly point this out, mentioning that your allocation to emerging markets might well have saved the portfolio during this miserable period. However, did anyone have the foresight to put as much as 50 percent of the portfolio in emerging markets at just the right time? Well, no. And we should point out that given the higher risk involved in investing in emerging markets, even the strongest advocates of diversified portfolios would scarcely recommend that you put any more than 10 percent of your portfolio in this risky asset class.

So the question becomes, How much did a 10 percent allocation to emerging markets help you during the period 2000–2009? It did help, but not very much, since you invested only 10 percent of your money in this asset class.

Much of the data in this chapter is derived from a section on the website *Mindfullyinvesting. com*, a site that I highly recommend. It was originated by Karl Steiner, a successful businessman who shares his own wisdom and investing theories on the site. I find the material to be very thoughtful and even provocative, and I think you will find it well worth a visit.

While I'm on the subject of useful sites, another one I recommend highly is *The Market Hustle*, which you can follow on Instagram. This very popular site offers thoughtful advice on investing and lifestyle that will be particularly helpful to young investors. The advice consists mainly of financial lifestyle exhortations, and they generally hit home. Here's an example: "Go broke buying assets to BECOME wealthy. Don't go broke buying luxuries to LOOK wealthy." There are also lots of specific, simple investment suggestions that make sense.

A few chapters from now, we'll go into detail on the construction and maintenance of your million-dollar portfolio.

CHAPTER ELEVEN

What If I Need Some of My Money before I Retire?

In the real world, most of us don't have the luxury of putting together a retirement account that we'll never need to call on before we actually retire. Fact of life. A typical list of the uses of retirement money before retirement might look like this:

- Children's education
- Temporary loss of income
- The down payment on a first or second home
- An extravagant vacation

With some additional imagination, you can add to this list. Most of us will need to plan to use some of our retirement money before we retire.

Consider the following: Let's assume that a portion of our savings fund will be needed during our lifetime for those extraordinary needs, such as those we have just listed. One way to handle this is to split our retirement money into two tranches. One piece, the larger one, will be the "untouchable" PEPP retirement fund, and another piece will grow alongside it but will be available for monetary needs that come along in life.

Remember that the investment strategy we recommend is one where we rely on the historic long-term appreciation of US stocks. If we dedicate a portion of our savings to a fund that we might need earlier than retirement, that fund should not be invested in the same manner as our long-term funds. This is simply because we may not be able to plan for the timing of our needed

> **If we dedicate a portion of our savings to a fund that we might need earlier than retirement, that fund should not be invested in the same manner as our long-term funds.**

additional funds. Now, some future needs can be planned for, such as the purchase of a house or condo and the children's college education. Other possible needs are more uncertain. In the case of the money for education, we can utilize 529 plans as an investment vehicle. Most states have 529 plans that allow you to save money in a tax-advantaged account for the kids' future education. The other funds will need to be invested in a manner to reduce the volatility that the longer-term funds may encounter.

These emergency funds will need to be invested in a lower-risk portfolio that will look like the long-term portfolio most investment advisors recommend. Back to square one! If you have an advisor, this is where he or she will be helpful. This pool of funds will be diversified to reduce high volatility. Like everything we've discussed so far, there is a reason for this. Since you don't know when you will need to use this pool of assets, it's important that you don't need them when the market is going through one of its temporary major setbacks. So for this part of the fund, you will reduce the equity portion of the portfolio to look more like the traditional 60/40 allocation of stocks and lower-risk assets like bonds, cash, preferred stocks, and gold. Most investment books over the years (including some of those I've written/cowritten) show how to build a balanced portfolio with dedicated features that help grow assets slowly with fewer ups and downs; however, your investment in pure equity will make far more money over the longer term.

With this said, for many investors, having two portfolios will be advisable. The main one will be the PEPP portfolio, which should grow your retirement assets into a multimillion-dollar nest egg. The second portfolio will be a pool of assets designed to fund shorter-term needs, as we have just discussed.

As I also mentioned, this shorter-term portfolio will be where a relationship with an investment advisor will be worth considering. Later on, we'll discuss other reasons to use an advisor once your portfolio and your age are at a point where your nest egg, now sufficiently large, will no longer be in a position to risk major market declines, however temporary.

The basic composition of this shorter-term portfolio may be as follows:

S&P 500 Index capitalization weighted	25%
S&P 500 Index equal weighted	25%
Gold	10%
Short-term bond fund:	40%
TOTAL	100%

The foregoing example is merely a sketch of what a traditional portfolio might look like. This is why I recommend using a professional investment advisor to help with this segment of your savings, should you decide you need it. Your advisor will recommend funds that suit your purpose and, more importantly, will be available to monitor these recommendations. This is not something we need to do in our basic retirement portfolio.

The question of what percentage of your savings should go into the retirement portfolio and what percentage into the shorter-term portfolio can't be answered universally. It will depend on several factors, including the visibility and timing of your future expenses (buying a house, saving for college, etc.). The amount you have available to save is another factor, which will of course vary from person to person. My hope is that you will save enough to put 80 percent of your savings into the long-term plan and 20 percent into the emergency fund, or numbers close to that. Assuming you are able to invest $1,000 to $3,000 a month, that should work.

CHAPTER TWELVE

Your Lifetime Pure Equity Plus Plan

As we have been discussing, the plan is simple. You make three purchases and rebalance the portfolio about once a year. Here are the specifics:

S&P 500 Index fund, SPY, capitalization weighted	45%
S&P 500 Index fund, RSP, equal weighted	45%
Gold, GLD	10%
TOTAL	100%

That is it—100 percent simple, elegant, and proven investment results.

Our suggested investment in gold shares is through GLD, the ETF that invests in and tracks the price of gold. Some investors may prefer to own the metal outright. That's okay if it makes you sleep better at night. In that case, buy gold coins or bars from a reputable dealer, and only pay a minimum fee over the market price of gold. You can compare dealer prices for gold at Comparegoldprices.com. Most investors buy the pretty one-ounce American Gold Eagle coins or the South African one-ounce Krugerrand. The United States Mint also sells gold coins but at collector prices at USmint.gov. Some gold-coin dealers will suggest that you buy gold collector coins, which sell at a considerable premium to the pure gold value of the coin. They will often back this suggestion up with a variety of studies that suggest that these coins increase in value more than the metal itself. Pay no attention. If you want to collect something, choose art, antiques, comic books, or anything else that strikes your fancy. (I collect modern first editions and have a very nice collection of Ernest Hemingway first editions and letters.) Just remember that you are not buying gold as a collector. You are buying gold as an investor, and you want to own the metal.

Now let's go back thirty-plus years to see how this portfolio would have performed under two sets of investment conditions. The investment results are for the portfolio we have recommended as detailed above. The first involves an initial investment of $10,000 back in 1990. We have compared the performance of that portfolio against other alternatives.

As you will see below, we are using data going back thirty-three years. Why that oddball number? For the S&P 500, we use total return data, reflecting dividends that are paid by the companies in the index. That's only fair. Although the S&P 500 Index goes back to 1957, the S&P 500 total return data (which includes dividends), as compiled by Bloomberg, only goes back to December 1987. So to reflect the results fairly, we begin with data from January 1988. Since our plan recommends that the investor make monthly contributions, we must calculate returns based on monthly data versus annual figures. Moreover, the monthly data for the Equal Weighted Index only began in December 1989, so for the years 1988 and 1989, we use the cap weighted-index and beginning in 1990, the data reflects the proposed 45% cap-weighted and 45% equal-weighted allocation plus 10 percent in gold.

Obviously, if we go back further, the results will be greater, and the advantage of the recommended portfolio will be even more striking. So if your savings timeframe is longer than thirty-three years, you can expect even higher results than these.

VALUE OF $10,000				
	Pure Equity Plus Portfolio	100 percent Equity Portfolio	100 percent Equity EW	100 percent Gold	60/40 Portfolio
1 Year	22,896.64	23,324.36	23,324.36	18,880.26	22,832.38
10 Years	324,724.86	375,082.53	357,548.37	98,134.54	299,791.54
15 Years	404,923.55	410,638.88	457,262.21	191,375.51	409,234.86
20 Years	894,938.55	829,327.98	1,037,483.81	564,420.14	719,692.59
30 Years	2,403,553.03	2,122,823.16	2,986,130.79	1,010,804.60	1,649,344.69
33 Years	3,431,658.26	3,174,642.51	4,036,878.26	1,486,234.36	2,258,054.34

Growth of $10,000 of a 90 percent Equity/10 percent Gold portfolio, starting January 1, 1988 through December 31, 1989. Thereafter, 45 percent Cap Weighted Equity, 45 percent Equal Weighted Equity, and 10 percent Gold.

$1,000 additional monthly contribution
Portfolio is rebalanced 1x per year

In this second chart, we assume an initial investment of $50,000 and a monthly contribution of $1,500 to your retirement portfolio.

VALUE OF $50,000				
	Pure Equity Plus Portfolio	100 percent Equity Portfolio	100 percent Equity EW	100 percent Gold	60/40 Portfolio
1 Year	74,043.19	75,800.04	75,800.04	57,981.09	73,840.69
10 Years	636,635.51	746,607.52	711,117.45	168,099.87	586,617.02
15 Years	769,286.98	794,610.18	882,193.88	312,226.97	774,700.48
20 Years	1,667,587.06	1,570,679.88	1,967,389.74	906,905.98	1,333,281.55
30 Years	4,391,939.75	3,922,645.78	5,560,337.38	1,610,398.19	2,985,068.57
33 Years	6,265,764.19	5,861,110.81	7,511,465.55	2,366,601.28	4,082,459.92

Growth of $50,000 of a 90 percent Equity/10 percent Gold portfolio, starting January 1, 1988 through December 31, 1989. Thereafter, 45 percent Cap Weighted Equity, 45 percent Equal Weighted Equity, and 10 percent Gold.

$1,500 additional monthly contribution
Portfolio is rebalanced 1x per year

Of course, there are endless number combinations of starting amounts and contribution amounts, but these two examples should help you understand the expected historic results for a large number of readers.

Let's now analyze the returns of this latter portfolio, where you begin with $50,000 and add $1,500 per month. In the preceding chart that begins in 1989, you learned that by following this plan for twenty years, your nest egg would have grown to $1.3 million using the standard 60/40 portfolio, where 60 percent of your assets were in equities and 40 percent in fixed income. And frankly, this result would have only been achieved if you had the wisdom to use index funds throughout instead of actively managed mutual funds, where your chances of underperforming the stock market were long. Moreover, this includes a period when bond yields were much higher than they are today.

Had you invested in the recommended portfolio, 90 percent equity and 10 percent gold, you would have $1.67 million in your retirement account.

It gets better.

Look at the thirty-three-year returns, where the 60/40 portfolio would have earned you about

$4 million while the recommended portfolio earned more than $6 million. Now, you'll probably also notice that had you been lucky enough to invest all your money in the equal-weighted S&P 500 Index, you would've wound up with a powerful nest egg of $7.5 million! No, we are not recommending that you do that, although if we were relying solely on a backtest to make recommendations, putting all your assets in that particular fund would have ended up at the top of the list. As we discussed earlier, backtests can be useful, but they do not dictate what an investor should do in the future. In this case, experience and sound judgment eclipse a pure backtest. True, the very long backtest proves that an investment in equity remains the best chance for increasing wealth historically. However, the combination of assets in the PEPP, with equity being the primary driver, is what I believe will offer the most rewarding outcome.

> **Set it and forget it, and rebalance about once a year to the original percentage allocations.**

There you have it. The Pure Equity Plus Plan that I recommend for your multimillion-dollar retirement. It is simple to implement, and once you put it on automatic investment in your 401(k) or Roth retirement account, the market will do the work for you. Set it and forget it, and rebalance about once a year to the original percentage allocations of 45 percent S&P 500 cap weighted, 45 percent to S&P 500 equal weighted, and 10 percent in gold.

A WORD ABOUT TAXES

I am not a CPA or tax advisor so I go out of my way to avoid giving tax advice with one exception which I will now share with you. Most investors save for retirement using a traditional IRA or 401(k) or both and there are variations of these for government employees or those who are self-employed. The way these plans work is that you contribute to them with pre-tax dollars and you don't pay taxes on the money you contribute, which makes them quite popular. However, when you withdraw your money starting at age 59 1/2, you pay taxes on the withdrawals.

There is another savings vehicle that works differently, and this is the one I recommend to you. It is the Roth IRA. Whereas with the traditional 401(k)s and IRAs you deduct the amount of your contribution from your taxes, the Roth IRA works the other way around: you contribute after-tax dollars and get no immediate tax deduction. The advantage is that you pay no taxes when you withdraw the money in retirement! This is such a huge advantage that we should be careful not to remind our legislators how great a benefit it is for taxpayers. As you can see from our projections of the growth of your savings, the amount of money you will likely have upon retirement will be in the millions of dollars. Obviously, paying the tax on the contribution and letting it grow tax-free is a major advantage over having to pay taxes on the amount you will have after your assets have grown over several decades. What this means is that the millions of dollars you will accumulate for retirement will be free of taxes when you take the money out, simply because you put it in a Roth IRA and paid the tax on your contributions which are about to grow substantially. There are other advantages to the Roth IRA that your tax advisor can share with you, but this tax advantage is so important, I wanted to be sure that you were aware of it.

CHAPTER THIRTEEN

Conclusion

We have come to the end of this short book that I expect will lead you to a rich retirement. But first, if you turned to this chapter without reading the book, please stop and go back. Read the entire book, or this summary will not be useful to you.

The Basic Premise

There are literally thousands of books on how to make money in the stock market. Every once in a while, one or two stand out and grab the attention of a large number of readers while the books fly off the shelves. I can name a few of these, and many are worth reading and following. Among the good ones, books by Peter Lynch are particularly noteworthy. Why? Because Peter Lynch has the record to prove what he is talking about. I interviewed him for my book *Investment Gurus*. Lynch was the legendary manager of the Fidelity Magellan Fund, where for thirteen years, from 1977 to 1990, he compiled a performance record that I believe will never be beaten. His performance record was to deliver an annual average return of 29 percent per year for thirteen years. I think I am safe in my belief.

In his books, Peter Lynch explains in great detail how he did it. No magic formulas, no hidden secrets, and he lays it all out for anyone to follow. In one case, he shares his analytical skills by telling the story of how his wife, Carolyn, came home from the supermarket one day with not only food but also a new pantyhose brand called L'eggs. Pantyhose for sale in the supermarket? She tried them on and loved them. Intrigued, Lynch did some quick calculations and figured out that if women started buying pantyhose in supermarkets, which the average woman visited ten times more often than the mall, that would make the product a huge success. He did some research and loaded up on the stock. It was one of his biggest winners.

So there you have it. Peter Lynch makes a fortune for his fund shareholders and tells you exactly how to do it in his three books. I recall that when I was touring with *Investment Gurus,* at my lectures in bookstores and on campuses, I would ask how many of the attendees had read any of Peter Lynch's books. Lots of hands went up. Then I asked how many people were getting rich after reading the books. Unfortunately, no hands went up. I wasn't surprised. You see, even though Peter Lynch told you how he did it, the difference between him and you is that he is Peter Lynch and you are not. His brain is wired differently from yours and mine, and he likely sees things we don't see.

There is a lesson here. When a great investor tells you how he became so successful, that does not mean you will duplicate his success by reading how he did it. It just doesn't work that way. So there must be another path to great wealth. That is what the book you just finished reading is about.

Here is the difference.

In guiding you to significant wealth for your retirement, I am relying on a long history of investment performance in the US stock market. We don't need to follow someone else's magic formula for investing. All we need to do is examine what has worked in the past and for how long it has worked. When we are satisfied that this trend is real, we follow it, along with a few tweaks that I added for additional safety and performance. If we are looking for a trend, one that is about a hundred years old certainly instills confidence.

As always, there is a catch. In this case, it requires that you execute the plan and not be overcome by fear when markets take a bad turn, which they inevitably will. The most important objective of this book is to convince you that you will recover from market meltdowns, given enough time. That is why the earlier you start on this journey, the richer you will become. Investors must have at least fifteen years left of saving and investing in their future well-being to profit from the advice given here. History is on your side.

Along the way, do not be tempted by stories about a mutual fund or some great money manager or broker who has had an amazing performance record. Even if true, that record will likely not be very long, perhaps a few years, and that kind of superperformance is indistinguishable between luck and skill. Rely instead on the very long history of performance of the American stock market. You don't need anything else. Remember: don't try to *beat* the market; *be* the market.

We have demonstrated in these pages that the simple path to wealth is with the US stock market. As part of this, we have added a small portion of gold to the Pure Equity Plus Plan as a

> **Don't try to beat the market; be the market.**

hedge against uncertainty and inflation. It should serve us well and not detract from the historic growth of US equities. As you begin, you can invest in the Pure Equity Plus Plan on your own. Some will find it useful to engage an advisor to help them along the way and to answer questions they might have. Once you have reached your desired retirement goal, a sum that should certainly be in the millions of dollars, you should then hire a professional investment advisor to allocate your assets—not for growth, but for safety. After you retire, you will no longer have enough runway to ride out any future Black Swan market events that may occur. At that point, you will have switched from a growth objective to a focus on preservation of capital, and an experienced investment advisor can help.

Let me leave you with the following statement by arguably the greatest investor in American history: Warren Buffett. I transcribed this, with some minor editing for clarity, from an interview he did in 2018 with Becky Quick of CNBC TV.

> *In 1942, when I bought my first stock, as an illustration of the things that have happened since 1942, we've had fourteen presidents, seven Republicans and seven Democrats. We've had world wars, we've had 9/11, we had the Cuban Missile Crisis, we've had all kinds of things. The best single thing you could have done on March 11, 1942, when I bought my first stock, was to buy an index fund and never look at the headlines, never think about stocks anymore, just like you would do if you bought a farm. Just buy the farm and let the tenant farmer run it for you. I pointed out that if you had put $10,000 in an index fund that reinvested dividends—and I pause for a moment here to let the audience try and guess how much it would amount to today. (short pause) It would come to $51 million. Wow. And the only thing*

you had to believe in then is that America would win the war and America would progress as it has ever since 1776. And if America moved forward, American business would move forward. You didn't have to worry about what stock to buy; you didn't have to worry what day to get in and out. You didn't know the Federal Reserve would exist, whatever it might be. America works.

Now, as we conclude our journey together, I wish you all the best in your pursuit of financial independence. In particular, I wish you courage and resolve; that is all it will take. So it is time to put the book down, grab your phone or laptop, and take the first step to gain control of your financial life and the financial freedom and independence that will follow.